DACHSHUND

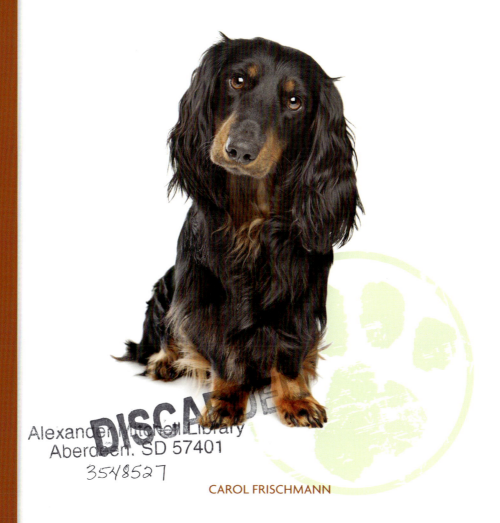

CAROL FRISCHMANN

Dachshund

Editor: Matthew Haviland
Indexer: Dianne L. Schneider
Designer: Angela Stanford
Series Designer: Mary Ann Kahn

TFH Publications®
President/CEO: Glen S. Axelrod
Executive Vice President: Mark E. Johnson
Publisher: Albert Connelly, Jr.
Associate Publisher: Stephanie Fornino

Marjorie Kaplan, President and General Manager, Animal Planet Media/Nicolas Bonard, GM & SVP, Discovery Studios Group/Robert Marick, VP, North American Licensing/Sue Perez-Jackson, Director, Licensing/Tracy Conner, Manager, Licensing

TFH Publications, Inc.®
One TFH Plaza
Third and Union Avenues
Neptune City, NJ 07753

Printed and bound in China

15 16 17 18 19 20 1 3 5 7 9 8 6 4 2

Library of Congress Cataloging-in-Publication Data
Frischmann, Carol.
  Dachshund / Carol Frischmann.
    pages cm. -- (Animal planet: Dogs 101)
  Includes bibliographical references and index.
  ISBN 978-0-7938-3734-2 (hardcover : alk. paper)
  1. Dachshunds. 2. Dogs. I. Title.
  SF429.D25F75 2015
  636.753'8--dc23
                            2014039265

This book has been published with the intent to provide accurate and authoritative information in regard to the subject matter within. While every reasonable precaution has been taken in preparation of this book, the author and publisher expressly disclaim responsibility for any errors, omissions, or adverse effects arising from the use or application of the information contained herein. The techniques and suggestions are used at the reader's discretion and are not to be considered a substitute for veterinary care. If you suspect a medical problem consult your veterinarian.

Note: In the interest of concise writing, "he" is used when referring to puppies and dogs unless the text is specifically referring to females or males. "She" is used when referring to people. However, the information contained herein is equally applicable to both sexes.

The Leader In Responsible Animal Care for Over 50 Years!®
www.tfh.com

CONTENTS

ORIGINS OF YOUR
DACHSHUND

Versatile in looks and talents, Dachshunds are playful and sometimes clownish companions and watchdogs, sure to alert you to passersby. Dachshunds bond very closely with "their people," becoming their shadows. They like other people, too, especially if they are well socialized as puppies, and can be good around children if children are a part of their socialization.

These loyal and persistent dogs don't all look alike. You can choose a Dachshund who is small with a wiry coat or larger with a long and silky coat—and all combinations. Whatever coat he has, the Dachshund is a skilled hunter of small vermin, rabbits, and underground game, including the badger. With his excellent nose, he can trail and track as well as follow game by sight.

Today, rather than badger or rabbit hunting, most members of this popular breed participate in sports and provide amusement and companionship to their families in city apartments, on farms, or in the suburbs. Lacking "doggy" odor, Dachshunds are clean house or apartment dogs, happy to be with their human families as long as they are walked often for exercise.

The development of the Dachshund from the earliest members of the dog family to the Dachsies we know today has been rapid since 1500 CE. What took quite a bit longer was the development of the domestic dog to the group of dogs that became hunting hounds.

Dachshunds are playful and sometimes clownish companions.

Dogs may have evolved from village-dwelling wolves who scavenged for human food.

DEVELOPMENT OF THE DOG

Dachshunds are members of the dog species (*Canis lupus familiaris*), which was domesticated from the gray wolf (*Canis lupus*). For many years, scientists thought that domestication of dogs occurred about 10,000 years ago. This was about the time that people in many parts of the world learned that they could store seeds from plants—barley, wheat, rice, and maize—and eat them over the winter, allowing humans to establish permanent villages.

However, recent evidence from DNA suggests that the relationship between humans and dog ancestors began 100,000 years ago, about the time modern people (*Homo sapiens*) evolved in Africa. For 80,000 to 90,000 years, perhaps human and wolf hunted as partners or lived loosely connected. However, because village-based agricultural humans needed vastly different qualities in a dog, the 10,000- to 20,000-year-ago period at which the physical attributes of dogs and wolves diverged markedly makes sense.

BECOMING HUMANKIND'S COMPANION

The process of dogs becoming humankind's helpmate is all guesswork. One common theory is that early peoples took wolf pups and trained them as hunting companions, beginning a long, slow process of taming. In contrast, behavioral scientists Raymond and Lorna Coppinger believe humans selecting, taming, and artificially breeding wolves is backward; more likely, they say, dogs arose via natural selection.

In other words, wolves of particular genetic groups took advantage of human food sources instead of hunting in packs. These groups then evolved to further take advantage of the steady food source and protection offered by living near humans. They adapted to scavenging, which would explain the development of dog-like traits, such as tameness and smaller heads and teeth.

The Coppingers believe that several factors helped mold the average village wolf-dog into specific breeds: natural selection and natural events (such as weather-related catastrophes), periodic canine plagues, and more recently, humans' intentional breeding of dogs to produce "breeds" with specific characteristics.

Certain wolves may have slowly evolved and developed dog-like traits, such as tameness and smaller heads and teeth.

EMERGING BREEDS

Developments in technology have allowed scientists to examine the genetic material of dogs to learn more about the origins of characteristics of groups and individual dogs. One study looked at the origin of short, curved legs, characteristic of today's Dachshunds, Basset Hounds, and at least 15 other breeds.

A single event appears to explain this characteristic. A mutation early in domestic dog development gave all short-legged breeds an extra copy of a gene that provides the directions for a growth-promoting protein. This extra gene creates a protein that turns on the growth receptors at the wrong time during fetal development, resulting in the group of short-legged breeds, including the Dachshund.

As early as 1400 BCE, carved metal objects portray small dogs that resemble the Dachshund. European illustrations created from 1400 to 1600 CE show long dogs with short legs and hound ears said to track like hounds and act like terriers, hunting badgers. About that same time, clay models of short-legged, long-bodied small dogs were discovered in Mexico. A 1580 woodcut by prominent Swiss printmaker Jost Amman shows a Miniature Dachshund–like dog hunting rabbits.

HISTORY OF THE DACHSHUND

The Dachshund Club of America Handbook on the Dachshund explains that exactly how the breed originated is not entirely clear. What *is* clear is that German breeders have had a major influence on the development of the breed. In fact, the German–English translation of "Dachshund" is "badger dog," a reminder that the breed was bred to hunt badgers.

As a part of the breed's development, Basset Hound genes may have been introduced to provide the capability to "go to ground"; if true, the incorporation of Basset Hound DNA helped provide the scent and earth capabilities that the Dachshund possesses today.

The German–English translation of "Dachshund" is "badger dog," a reminder that the breed was bred to hunt badgers.

GERMAN BADGER DOG

Much of the Dachshund's characteristics come from the 1700s, when German hunters focused on the development of dogs who could be used to hunt badgers and boar and a second strain of dogs who were suitable for hunting fox and hare. The larger dogs, who were 30 to 35 pounds (13.5 to 16 kg), worked the larger game, while the smaller dogs, about 10 pounds (4.5 kg) lighter, made better harriers. These strains would become the Standard and Miniature Dachshunds.

By the 1800s, the Dachshund was a recognized breed in Germany, with the short-coated dog developing first. The alternative coat types came from outcrossing with other breeds to develop first the Longhaired and more recently the Wirehaired varieties.

DACHSHUNDS GAIN INTERNATIONAL ACCLAIM

During the 1800s, the Dachshund breed became popular in Germany, and the first standard for the breed was written there. In addition, the breed's popularity began to rise outside Germany. Queen Victoria popularized the Dachshund in England; from England, the little dog's popularity spread to America.

The Dachshund Club of America (DCA) was formed in 1895, and by 1914, the Westminster Kennel Club Dog Show featured many Dachshunds. Of course,

Dachshunds achieved international popularity during the 1800s.

One of the pleasures of having dogs is talking about the funny moments, and the loving moments, in your lives together.

during World War I, Dachshunds, like everything German, became unpopular. After the war, their popularity slowly rebuilt.

DACHSHUND BREED CLUBS

Dachshund breed clubs exist in many different countries. The DCA and the National Miniature Dachshund Club (NMDC) are two American Dachshund clubs. Dachshund breed clubs also exist under the aegis of the Kennel Club (KC) in Britain and the Federation Cynologique Internationale (FCI), or the World Canine Organization, which recognizes Germany as the "owner" country of the Dachshund. Each of these organizations has published breed standards, endorses breed clubs, and holds competitions whose champions are recorded in the organizations' studbooks.

DACHSIES IN POPULAR CULTURE

Most Dachshunds are famous in their own families. In fact, once you've had a Dachshund, you may find it difficult to imagine having a different breed of dog. One of the pleasures of having dogs is to talk about the funny moments, as well as the loving moments, in your lives together. These are the stories that we tell again and again about these great friends.

ORIGINS OF YOUR DACHSHUND

You're more likely to find modern Dachshunds tunneling under sheets and blankets than through badger dens.

Some Dachshunds become famous because they're owned by someone famous. Personalities as different as Queen Victoria, Fergie of the Black Eyed Peas, and Picasso have owned Dachshunds. Other Dachshund people include John F. Kennedy, who traveled with his dog Dunker in Europe, and singer Adele, who has Louie. John Wayne's wiener dog, Blackie, is said to have awakened the family, allowing them to escape from a fire. The mysterious Andy Warhol had the Dachsie Archie. It's also said that Napoleon Bonaparte, early in his career as a general, had Dachshunds, too.

Dachshunds are fixtures in American pop culture. Their nicknames include wiener dog, frankfurter dog, hot dog, Dachshie, sausage, bratwurst, and schnitzel. People love to dress their Dachshunds, especially their Miniature Dachshunds, and costumes seem popular on Halloween and for other holidays.

WHAT'S NEXT FOR BREED DEVELOPMENT?

From the human desire to have more novelty in "man's best friend," the number of dog breeds is increasing. Based on DNA analysis, scientists have determined that modern dogs are descended from four categories of dogs: wolf-like, herders, hunters, and Mastiff-like. These four groups of dogs evolved into the many breeds recognized today (more than 500 recognized by registries worldwide) by variation in only a few genes.

Unlike most mammals (including humans), who require hundreds of genes to interact to produce a visible inherited characteristic, dogs require about three. Three important genes control coat, size, and leg length. This means that by using small numbers of animals, great genetic variability can be expressed. As a result, the look of dogs changes rapidly over a small number of generations.

Breeds look as they do because a "registering agency" sets a breed standard on which registry judges base their awards of merit. Breeders plan matings based on the standard to produce dogs who match the standard as closely as possible.

As humans quest for "the novel," new breeds representing new looks, based on the variations provided by this small number of genes, are being added to registries in increasing numbers. In the last several years, for example, the AKC has added the American English Coonhound, the Portuguese Podengo Pequeno, and the Xoloitzcuintli (pronounced "show-low-eats-queen-tlee") as new breeds. Others are "in the wings," becoming new breeds.

The principle illustrated is that as dog fanciers become interested in a particular look and temperament, a "breed" is developed. But for now, our Dachshund is as the registries describe it—the descendent of badger hunters. Although some Dachshunds still hunt game today, you're more likely to find the breed tunneling under sheets and blankets, hunting for a more comfortable place to snooze on their person's bed.

CHAPTER 2

CHARACTERISTICS OF YOUR DACHSHUND

Dachshunds have powerful personalities and long lives, many reaching 12 to 14 years of age.

T he Dachshund's history as a dog meant to drag badgers from their dens and track wounded game molded the physical type and personality of the breed. Both physical and behavioral traits are largely inherited characteristics, ones that cannot be changed or modified through training. This is the reason why people new to a breed are advised to choose their dog based on the breed's temperament and physical attributes—to ensure that they're getting a dog who suits their family's lifestyle and personality.

Dachshunds have powerful personalities and long lives, many reaching 12 to 14 years of age, but they fall in the middle of the scale for exercise requirements, friendliness to people and other dogs, and trainability. Some Dachshunds continue as working game dogs for subsistence hunters, sportspeople, and those who make their living eliminating nuisance vermin. However, far more have jobs as faithful pets and excellent watchdogs. Sometimes they also compete as athletes, proving their DNA still powers their ability as versatile hunters and trackers, even as breeders add colors and markings to suit the public's fondness for new looks.

PHYSICAL DESCRIPTION

In accordance with American Kennel Club (AKC) standards, the Dachshund's personality and body type suit the nature of a hunter of badgers. The badger is known as a short-tempered, aggressive animal weighing about 25 pounds (11.5 kg). Even facing this angry meat eater with 1-1/2-inch (4-cm) claws, Dachshunds are fearless fighters who make decisions on their own, are more persistent than their enemies are, and show bravery in pursuing their game.

Like the emotional nature of this dog, his physicality has also been formed by his work. Think of what bodily attributes would help a dog who plunges into a tunnel and digs relentlessly to reach an opponent with large teeth and claws. Compact, loose skinned, muscular, and solid are some of the characteristics you can imagine, and these are the basic traits of the Dachshund physique.

If you consider his history and his other uses—tracking by scent, rabbiting, and watchdogging—you may imagine that some variation in the breed has occurred. Two sizes, three varieties, and many coat color and pattern combinations create differences in appearance that are somewhat astonishing.

Dog Tale

Several authors of varying types have included Dachshunds in their writing. For alternative points of view, consider reading their personal perspectives about Dachshunds. Here are four authors—two who include Dachshunds in their mystery novels, one in his serious fiction, and one in his essays.

• Just as Dachshunds can be a mystery, Dachshunds can also help solve mysteries, as they do in several series. Two Dachshund detectives are Rita Mae Brown's Wirehaired wiener dog Baxter from *A Nose for Justice* and Maxie McNabb's Miniature Dachshund Stretch from Sue Henry's Maxie and Stretch Mystery series.

• With *Randy Lopez Goes Home: A Novel*, Rudolfo Anaya dreams up a novel of the cultures and peoples of the American Southwest. The Dachshund Oso accompanies the title character in this short and challenging book about healing.

• E. B. White (of *Charlotte's Web* fame) said that his Dachshund, Fred, had the "look of fake respectability." To find out more about Fred, try *Essays of E. B. White*, several of which feature the author's Dachshund.

GENERAL BODY DESCRIPTION

The Dachshund is long bodied and low to the ground, suitable for passing through dense underbrush and into small tunnels. His skin is elastic and pliable without wrinkling. The overall impression is of a powerfully built dog, very strong for his size.

HEAD

The Dachshund's elongated face tapers to the tip of his slightly arched nose. Dark, almond-shaped eyes look energetic beneath prominent bridge bones. Rounded ears set near the top of the head frame his face, collect scent from the ground, and funnel it to his nose. His powerful jaws contain strong teeth and hinge well behind the eyes, teeth fitting closely together in a scissors bite. His long, muscular neck fits gracefully into the shoulders without making a sharp angle.

BODY

The Dachshund's well-muscled body has what's referred to as a "wraparound" front because his front legs literally wrap around his forechest, resulting in legs that are as close to the body as possible. This also means that the legs take

Dachshunds' compact, muscular bodies help them propel through heavy soil.

minimum space and produce maximum power. His strong shoulders, short front legs, and broad front feet are especially effective for digging.

The Dachshund's hindquarters not only fold compactly, but they also provide the force to propel the dog forward through tunnels, even as he is digging through heavy soil. This results from the thigh and calf being equally long and joined at a 90-degree angle to provide great driving power.

The deep chest and the well-rounded ribs provide the hardworking heart and lungs with the space they need for expansion during tunneling in an oxygen-depleted den. The after-chest and keel are long and provide protection for the organs. The tail, a continuation of the spine, is straight.

SIZE

Even the largest Standard Dachshund weighs only about 30 pounds (13.5 kg), so the breed is small. In the United States, Dachshunds come in two sizes: Standards weigh from 16 to 32 pounds (7.5 to 14.5 kg) and Miniatures ideally weigh 11 pounds (5 kg) or less.

The German Dachshund registry separates competition sizes by chest circumference rather than by weight, resulting in three sizes based on the size of the hole the dog can enter when "going to ground." Therefore, sizes are determined by chest circumference just under the elbows. Those more than 13 8/10 inches (35 cm) are Standards, and those from 11 8/10 to 13 8/10 inches (30 to 35 cm) are Miniatures. The smallest Dachshund size in Germany, the Rabbit Dachshund, has a chest circumference less than 11 8/10 inches (30 cm).

COAT

The three varieties of Dachshund coats—smooth, wirehaired, and longhaired—have all the basic attributes of the Dachshund's basic body type and a few special attributes expressed through their coats.

- The Smooth Dachshund has a short coat with smooth, shiny hair.
- The Wirehaired Dachshund is covered with a short, thick outercoat with finer, shorter undercoat. His distinctive face has a beard and eyebrows, and the hair covering the ears is shorter than on the body. The tail is thickly haired, tapering to a point. Wirehaired Dachshunds, probably crossbred with various terrier-type dogs, have a coat that protects them against thick underbrush.
- Many people believe that the luscious, wavy coat of the Longhaired Dachshund may have come from crossbreeding with spaniels. It afforded hunting Dachshunds more warmth than the smooth coat, but like the wirehaired coat, could become matted with burrs and mud.

COLORS

Colors, color mixes, and markings can become complicated because of the genetics involved. Some color traits are dominant, meaning they need be present in only one parent to be expressed. Some color traits and markings are recessive, meaning they need to be present in both parents to be expressed. Some color traits and markings are the result of mixtures of dominant and recessive genes. Your breeder will know about the genetics of your particular dog.

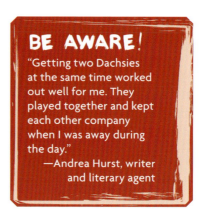

BE AWARE!

"Getting two Dachsies at the same time worked out well for me. They played together and kept each other company when I was away during the day."
—Andrea Hurst, writer and literary agent

Colors, Color Mixes, and Markings in Dachshunds

Single Colors	Black, chocolate, cream, fawn (also called Isabella), red, wheaten, wild boar
Color Mixes	Black & cream, black & tan, blue & cream, blue & tan, chocolate & cream, chocolate & tan, fawn & cream, fawn & tan
Markings	Brindle, brindle piebald (usually from puppy mills, as AKC or reputable breeders do not double patterns), dapple (merle), double dapple (ear or eye defects common), piebald (often not accepted as AKC standard), sable

YOUR DACHSHUND'S BACK

For those many Dachshunds who have not been bred with health in mind, and even for some who have been carefully bred and have unfortunate luck, a Dachshund's back can be very delicate and susceptible to injury. With their background as diggers and fierce hunters—their superior athleticism—you wouldn't guess this.

As many as one-quarter of all Dachshunds will develop back trouble sometime in their lives, starting between three and seven years of age. Typically, the cushioning disks between the vertebrae (or the pieces of the backbone) lose their resilience and no longer work as shock absorbers. Forces on the spine, especially twisting forces, can exert pressure on part of a disk, causing the disk to rupture.

When this happens, the material inside the disk bulges, compressing the spinal cord and causing pain or paralysis. Most cases occur in the lower back. Expensive surgery may be required. If you wonder why people take a chance on a dog who might need expensive care, any Dachshund lover will tell you, "Because they're worth it."

Unless your veterinarian advises otherwise, avoid having your Dachshund do things that strain his neck and back. No jumping up and down, no long flights of stairs, and no tug-of-war. There will be more on this topic in Chapter 6.

PERSONALITY

The Dachshund might be described as a small working hound with the personality of a terrier. Lively dogs, they enjoy as much exercise as you can give them. However, they love to sit on your lap while you read or lie on their backs snoozing while you watch television. Loyal companions, they can make good family pets and have a penchant for cleanliness.

The Longhaired is the gentlest variety, with a spaniel-type disposition, soft and sweet. The Wirehaired's personality is part terrier, part clown. The Smooth is a combination of the Longhaired and the Wirehaired. No matter their coat type,

Dachsies are small working hounds with the personality of a terrier.

keep in mind that Dachshunds are hounds, a group not known for obedience—they're easily distracted by an inviting scent, for example. Nevertheless, a patient and persistent companion can live harmoniously with her Dachshund.

The best person to own a Dachshund is gregarious and has a good sense of humor. She can take charge and is willing to train her dog and make it fun. She chooses activities that include her dog. Preferring to be the center of attention, Dachshunds benefit from participation in activities such as hunting, canine freestyle (doggy dancing), obedience, and therapy dog programs.

Dachshunds do not like being left alone for long periods; once his owner comes home, the Dachshund expects to be the center of attention.

COMPANIONABILITY

Although extroverted and bold, Dachsies prefer their family to meeting new people. If you have children, however, be sure that your Dachshund is already accustomed to them. Not every breed or every individual within a breed appreciates the finer qualities of small people who do unpredictable things. And both Dachshunds and children can be quite stubborn.

While adults understand how to gain the dog's cooperation—wear the hat and I'll give you a treat—small children simply swoop down on the little fellow with a Superman cape and shouts of glee. Some Dachsies do not enjoy the antics of children.

By the way, Dachshunds are not particularly warm to strangers. For this reason, your Dachshund will alert you to neighborhood activities and people unfamiliar to him. Once you introduce the stranger, your Dachshund should accept her, happy to be the center of attention again.

Dachshunds live happily with other Dachshunds. They often enjoy being two to a family. Typically, they can tolerate other breeds too, but in order to tolerate cats, they need to be raised with cats from puppyhood.

ENVIRONMENT

Dachshunds are adaptable to country life, life in the suburbs, or life as an apartment dog. Because they come in two sizes, you can select the size that fits your space. You might consider the

Dog Tale

"My friends call my Wirehaired Dachshund Desi 'The Sheriff,' because like a typical Dachsie, he is all noise and bravado when they arrive, then quickly becomes their best friend once they are sniffed and approved."

—Terry Albert, Pet Portraits, Poway, CA

individual dog's temperament when looking for an apartment or suburban dog. Dachshunds have a sharp bark. Further, all dogs, but young dogs in particular, need supervision and exercise. Without those, barking resulting from pent-up anxiety and boredom can create problems with neighbors in close quarters.

Stairs are not a good idea for Dachshunds. In fact, many owners install ramps to prevent back strain from the repeated jarring of their long backs and short legs navigating stairs or jumping onto and off of furniture.

EXERCISE REQUIREMENTS

Dachshunds, particularly as they age, tend to put on weight as their companions feed them treats. Because of the chance of back trouble with Dachshunds, keeping them slim lessens the chance of painful problems. For this reason, adequate exercise is a must.

This doesn't mean running miles each day. One or two brisk walks daily for 20 or 30 minutes are good for the Dachsie's health (and his companion's). Dachshunds enjoy brisk walks and do not require a yard for exercise. In fact, wherever you live, these dogs would prefer to take their exercise with you.

TRAINABILITY

All dogs are trainable; the question is whether you have the skills to train your dog. Dachshunds are not a breed that a first-time dog owner should train without experienced assistance. This brings up another important question:

CHARACTERISTICS OF YOUR DACHSHUND

whether you understand your breed well enough to do the training without help.

We know that Dachshunds are hunters. They have digging in their genes. They also like clowning and being the center of attention; if there is anything a Dachshund hates, it is being ignored. Finally, they are stubborn. Dachshunds do very little that they do not want to do. You must use these tendencies to create training that seems like a game.

Walking your Dachshund once or twice daily for 20 or 30 minutes keeps him healthy.

The second part of training is to manage your own expectations. Here are two examples of things you should expect from your Dachshund-in-training:

1. Few people will ever train a Dachshund well enough to let him off-leash in a city park. The "thinking part" of the Dachshund brain shuts down when squirrel scent hits his nose, releasing chemicals into the bloodstream that urge, "Run, run, run after that squirrel as if your life depends on it."

2. You probably cannot train your Dachsie not to dig. Certainly, you should not expect any fence to hold him unless you have wire buried a foot (30.5 cm) deep, and even then you won't be sure. Your Dachshund is bred to dig, and no amount of positive reinforcement for not digging will hold back his instinct when moles tunnel outside his fence, taunting him. Your dog is going to get that mole wherever he is, including under the fence. The same is true if you have mice in your basement or garage. The door between your dog and the mouse is history.

To train your Dachshund successfully, you must love him for what he is and not expect what is impossible. If these characteristics make you question whether the Dachsie is the breed for you, then it is not the breed for you.

DACHSHUND

GROOMING REQUIREMENTS

Grooming is not just about appearance. Grooming is also about health and bonding. It's about health because you're checking over your dog as you groom him, removing ticks, feeling for lumps and bumps. You'll notice if his stomach is tender. It's about bonding because you're spending time together, doing something that feels good to your dog and for you.

- Smooth Dachshunds require the least grooming because their coats are short. A weekly grooming with a soft-bristle brush will keep their coats in good condition.
- Wirehaired Dachshunds need frequent brushing to remove the remains of their forays into the fields. During molting season, when dogs are said to "blow their coat," removing the loose dead hair is important for keeping Dachsie looking good. Use a brush with short wire bristles and remember that trimming maintains the classic look of the coat.
- Longhaired Dachshunds require regular brushing, followed by combing to remove mats. Mats may need to be untangled by hand.

Brushing removes the hair that will otherwise be shed indoors. Although brushing does not stop your Dachsie from shedding, it does reduce the amount of hair distributed on the furniture. Regular brushing and combing also keep the Wirehaired and Longhaired varieties from dreading a "big" grooming, which if delayed too often, can be a long process.

For novices, consultation with an experienced groomer is a good way to learn not only how to do the grooming but also how to gain cooperation in this regular part of a dog's life. Learn more about grooming in Chapter 5.

PUPPY POINTER

"If your puppy likes toys, dangle a favorite pull toy to try to engage him in walking on the leash. If he's all about food, try using aerosol cheese or peanut butter on a long-handled kitchen spoon to entice him to walk next to you on the leash. Don't ask for too much too soon; puppies have very short attention spans, so if he walks a few steps with you, tell him he's wonderful and don't ask for more than that . . . gradually work your way up to a full-fledged walk on a leash, but be patient."

—Holly Deeds, Dachshund trainer and teacher, Chattanooga, TN, and her heavily titled pack: FC Duchwood Great Expectations ("Stella"); FC Doxikota Our Mutual Friend ("Jenny"); and Doxikota's Copperfield Miss ("Lark")

SUPPLIES FOR
YOUR DACHSHUND

A basket with a soft liner can make for a good Dachshund daybed.

upplies for your Dachshund don't need to be expensive or specially made. They simply must be durable and of reasonable quality. In general, buying fewer products, of higher quality, will pay off in the long run.

BED

Although many people allow their dogs to sleep in bed with them or family members, I recommend that dogs sleep in their crates. Both person and dog will have a better night's sleep, and you will be spared the irritation of cleaning hair from your every nook and cranny or the anguish of a ruined mattress if your dog has an accident. In addition, crates are the modern household version of a den, the place that dogs naturally go to sleep.

To transform a crate to a bed, line the bottom with a comfy towel or washable blanket. Use several if you like. If you wish to purchase a "daybed" for your dog, a basket with a towel liner is a good choice, and a hard plastic bed with a towel liner is an excellent choice. Fancy beds are not a good investment. The first time your dog is irritated, the fancy bed may be chewed beyond recovery.

CLOTHING

If you have no mudroom in which to dry and clean your dog (or no inclination to do so), consider rain gear as a way to make reentry less messy than one would expect with a sopping wet Dachshund dashing about from couch to chair.

Do take advantage of opportunities to keep your Dachshund dry and sweet smelling, but be careful that he doesn't overheat in close-fitting clothing. Dogs' natural fur coats protect them in all but the most awful weather.

COLLAR AND HARNESS

Purchase a flat nylon adjustable buckle collar on which your Dachsie's tags can hang. These are the tags with your telephone number. Some people also include the dog's name, the family's name, and their address.

The average Standard Dachshund neck size is 16 to 20 inches (40.5 to 51 cm) and the average Miniature Dachshund neck size is 8 to 18 inches (20.5 to 45.5 cm), but measure your dog for the best fit—you should be able to place two fingers between the collar and his neck. He should always wear this collar for identification purposes.

You can also purchase a harness for your Dachshund for walks. Some people prefer a harness rather than a leash and collar. A harness can keep the pressure from your dog's neck if your dog is not trained well enough that he does not pull. Because Dachsies are prone to neck and back problems, you might discuss this choice with your breeder and a veterinarian.

A variety of harness styles exist, including those made particularly for Dachshunds. Be sure to consider, if they are the vest-type harness, that the fabric is breathable and can easily be dried to allow your dog to be comfortable even on wet days.

Because Dachsies are prone to neck and back problems, consider walking your dog with a harness.

Keep in mind that Dachshunds have a unique head shape; often their necks are larger than their heads. If your Dachsie pulls forward, he puts pressure on his neck; if he pulls backward, his head may slip free of his collar. Martingale collars were designed to prevent both these problems. These collars have a large loop to which the leash is attached, which keeps the collar taut on the neck. The other loop allows you to adjust the collar to fit your dog.

Martingale collars may be best for walking Dachsies.

However, if your dog frequently pulls forward, straining on the leash, try a head halter or a harness, because you don't want his neck or back strained. Some head collars have the advantage of giving you control of your dog's head. Of course, never pull or tug on your dog's neck when using any collar or harness.

CRATE

Crates are substitute dog dens. They are places where your dog can go and have peace and quiet; he can relax there and know that no one in the family will enter his "sacred space." Your job is to make sure that your dog's view of his crate remains that way.

Never let a child or another dog play inside your dog's crate. Never bother your dog while he is there. As when you need time alone, your dog will retreat to his safe space. For you, the crate also becomes a place where you can protect your dog from disturbance or harm. For example, when you need to leave the house—a place full of hazards for an unsupervised, untrained new dog or puppy—the crate is a protector. When you travel, your dog's home goes with him.

Crates are made of wire and of plastic. Plastic crates are good for travel in cold weather or for keeping your dog's space especially private. It's hard to see or poke through plastic. Wire crates allow more airflow and therefore cooling in hot areas. Your dog can be separated from the family or the potential danger but still see and feel a part of the activities.

A compromise is a wire crate that comes with a cloth cover. You get the advantages of wire (easy to clean, chew-resistant, and cool in the summer) with the advantages of plastic (privacy and warmth). The one place this won't work is if you have to ship your dog in an airplane.

HOW MANY?

Many people enjoy the use of two crates for their dog: one for home use, one for car travel. Wire crates work well for the latter because you can see your dog and your dog can see you. And the temperature stays about the same as your moving car.

PUPPY POINTER

While your Dachsie is a puppy, consider purchasing or borrowing a second crate. Put one in your kitchen. While you're preparing and cooking food, the crate allows Dachsie to spend time with you but keeps you and Dachsie safe while you're chopping and handling hot pots and pans.

CRATE OR DOG BED?

For the first year, place a crate rather than a dog bed in your bedroom. Initially, buy a heavy plastic crate for this purpose. This more den-like enclosure provides a cozy atmosphere and privacy. And if your puppy does potty in his crate, your bedroom floor will be protected. Once he is an adult, you can make a lovely cover for this unattractive piece of furniture or sell the crate and purchase a pleasant-looking or coordinating dog bed.

CRATE SIZE

Every puppy needs a crate. What's not obvious when your puppy is tiny is that he's going to grow and to need a larger crate. Size your crate for your puppy's projected adult size. Many crates have a panel that you can insert to partition the space as your puppy grows. This is necessary because if the crate is too large, a puppy may use one end for sleeping and the other end as a toilet. Your breeder can give you advice about the size she expects your puppy to reach as an adult.

CRATE BEDDING

Bedding for the crate can be a blanket or a large soft towel on top of a slip-proof mat. Use old blankets, large fabric scraps sold on clearance at fabric stores, and towels until your puppy outgrows the chewing stage. Then you can buy beautiful bedding if you'd like.

EXERCISE PEN

Exercise pens were developed for competition dogs to have a place to exercise, to potty, and to relax outside of their crates. These wire or galvanized-steel enclosures come in different sizes with interlocking panels. Invest in an exercise pen, or "ex-pen," and use it like a playpen. Get one with a gate panel that is large enough and sturdy enough to withstand your dog's full adult height and weight.

An exercise pen not only works for puppyhood but also works for the rest of your lives together. It is incredibly useful when you travel with your Dachshund and for nursing care whenever your Dachshund needs it.

FOOD AND WATER BOWLS

Use stainless-steel food and water bowls. You'll want dishwasher-safe bowls, probably two of each. That way, you have one set in the dishwasher and the other set in use. If you don't wish to purchase the weighted stainless bowls that your Dachshund will not be able to overturn, then purchase a properly sized crock instead.

Choose a size in proportion to your Dachshund. If you purchase bowls about the size of your dog's head, you've got the right size. Using too large a bowl promotes water-related mischief. You may want to purchase a package of scrunchies or fabric hair bands to keep your Dachshund's ear hair clear of his food bowl, if he wears it long.

For those Dachsie owners worried about bloat, there are bowls that "slow down" the dog's eating. Rather than using those, you might want to simply spread out your dog's food on the floor and make him travel to reach it. Alternatively, put the food in a treat that dispenses small amounts as your dog moves the ball.

GATE

A baby gate, intended for human children, is an excellent investment if you have a set of stairs or a room that you want to deny access to. Or perhaps you want to use the gate as a barrier to keep your Dachsie in the mudroom until his paws are clean. These gates are excellent tools for keeping your house clean and your dog safe from things that could be harmful.

GROOMING SUPPLIES

The following are the basic grooming supplies you'll need for your Dachsie:
• dog shampoo
• dog toothpaste
• ear cleaner
• heavy-duty emery board

- nail clippers (guillotine type)
- narrow-toothed comb
- rubber mat in the bottom of the bathtub or sink to provide sure footing for the dog
- pin brush
- slicker brush
- styptic powder (in case you cut a nail quick)
- towels
- wide-toothed comb
  and, for longhaired and wirehaired coats,
- electric clipper with #10 blade, #5 blade, #7 blade
- scissors
- stripping blade

IDENTIFICATION

Your telephone number and your Dachshund's name should be on a tag that you attach to his collar. Never remove his flat collar—you never know when something unexpected will happen.

In addition, your veterinarian will offer to microchip your dog. A small tag is inserted under the skin between the shoulder blades during a routine veterinary visit—most likely your initial health exam. The microchip can help a shelter or a veterinarian identify your dog in the event that his collar is lost, which can make all the difference in getting him back.

LEASH

You need at least one leash, and two is better—keep one at home and one in the front seat of your car as a safety precaution for you and your constant companion. The best purchase is a 6-foot (2-m) leash. Most dog people prefer a

Dog Tale

As a frequent dog sitter for Dachsies, I was astonished by the strength of their pull against the leash. Most Dobermans I've cared for don't pull that hard. When a dog is determined to pull against the leash, I think two things: (1) get a harness, right away, and (2) start retraining the dog to walk properly on a leash. Straining the neck, back, and shoulders can hasten expensive and difficult back troubles for these wonderful dogs.

leather leash (also called a "lead") because it is hard-wearing and a good value.

You may also want to invest in a second, "hands-free" leash, which joggers wear with their dogs. Even if you don't plan to run with your Dachshund, you might decide to attach your new dog to your side while you do chores. This is one of the best ways to exercise your dog as well as to accustom a new dog to following you, and not the other way around. Besides, a hands-free leash gives you—well—free hands.

RAMPS AND STAIRS

Ramps for car access and stairs to reach the sofa or bed are necessities for older dogs with delicate backs. You can create your own ramps with plywood and molding strips or you can purchase them in pet stores and online. A complete list of back support tools is available from Dodgerslist (dodgerslist.com).

TOYS

If you don't provide enough toys, Dachsies will make toys of your possessions. These are busy dogs who need something to do. Toys have different purposes: teething, indoor playtime, boredom relief, and exercise.

CHEW TOYS

Toys to chew come in many different types. There are, of course, the "made from materials that resist bullets" sorts of toys. These are the ones that hold up best, even though they are expensive. Find the small toys made of this very durable material. You'll find these quality toys have no small parts that your Dachsie can pull off and swallow.

Other sorts of chew toys are meant to "give" a bit when they are chewed. These might be best for your teething puppy. Remember, they have sharp teeth and are growing a set of their adult teeth. Provide lots of these to help your puppy through the teething stage; your shoes and furniture legs will thank you.

Whatever sort of chew toy you purchase, avoid toys that are cute for you but are manufactured cheaply, with materials that might be swallowed, such as moveable eyes, buttons, bells, etc. Although the toys are inexpensive, the veterinary bill will not be. Don't take a chance with your beloved companion.

SQUEAKY TOYS

Squeaky toys are fun to chew and to pounce on. Again, the quality of the manufacturing is key to the toy's safety. Find well-crafted, hefty, rubber-like toys with the squeak buried deep inside. As the toy becomes worn and the "squeak"

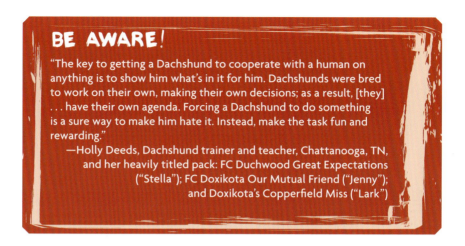

part can possibly be extracted and swallowed, throw it away and get another one. Examples include balls with squeaks, well-crafted mice, or those "made from fabric that stops bullets" toys. Get the appropriate size for your Dachsie's mouth. Buy two of each and store one as a replacement.

STUFFABLE TOYS

Edible toys are a great option when your dog needs occupying in his ex-pen. These toys are created to be stuffed with kibble or peanut butter. They are shaped like bee hives, balls, bones, and pull toys. Again, go for the quality.

In addition to different sizes, manufacturers list the "different bite strengths" on the labels. You need a toy that is durable but not one that is sized and hard enough for a giant Mastiff.

INTERACTIVE TOYS

When you want to play with your dog, these are good toys to use. Take one or two outside with you during outdoor playtime. Tennis balls or balls that are more durable but look and bounce like tennis balls are excellent. Frisbee look-alikes that your Dachsie can chase after and bring back for more fun are excellent. You'll also want some highly durable toys you can bury in your dig pit. If you have a very durable stick for tossing, that might keep your Dachsie retrieving for hours.

Recently, makers have produced toys that dogs can activate themselves through motion. Keep track of the latest in technology for new developments for your Dachsie. An excellent place for more information is a Listserv that specializes in Dachshunds.

FEEDING YOUR DACHSHUND

Figuring out what to feed your Dachshund can be confusing, as there's a bewildering array of choices on the market. "Experts" blog, in minute detail, about the vast array of supplements they deem critical to your dog's health. Meanwhile, your best friend makes her own raw diet and wants you to join the cooperative to purchase meat in bulk. About the time that you decide that she's right, you see a commercial for prepackaged gourmet dog dinners you'd like to eat yourself. Most of what you're seeing and hearing is either a well-intentioned alternative to marketing fluff or actual marketing fluff. After reading this chapter, you'll be able to tell the difference.

Let's take a painless look at nutrition basics. Then we'll go on a virtual tour of the commercial dog food market and contrast that with the home-prepared diets that the dog world's Martha Stewarts do so well. You'll learn whether gourmet diets are worth the cost, when you should use supplements, and the best ideas for treats. You'll also learn how much of the dog population is overweight, why that matters, and what the right weight for your dog looks like.

One important point often overlooked about diets is, "If your dog is doing well, how bad can the diet be?" Dogs sometimes do well on diets you wouldn't think were very good. One way to evaluate your Dachsie's diet is to simply observe his body condition (and your veterinarian does this at your annual exam). How do his

Commercial dog food offers a wide array of choices.

coat, eyes, and teeth look? What is his energy level? If he looks good and he feels good, his diet is probably good too.

WHY GOOD NUTRITION IS ESSENTIAL

Good nutrition complements your Dachshund's healthy genes and temperament. A well-nourished dog feels good and looks good. He has energy; not that you won't wish sometimes that he had a little less energy, but he's that muscular, well-balanced, curious, smart son of a gun you love. Good nutrition will keep him feeling and looking good for much longer than he would otherwise live.

Fine nutrition helps stave off disease activated by a poor diet. It builds the body in the best manner possible so that bones, joints, and the nervous system work the way they should. Good nutrition means that your Dachshund is never too hungry and never worried about the availability of food. It's there. It tastes good. It doesn't make his digestive system work too hard.

With a good diet, food breaks down and your Dachshund can eliminate wastes easily. As a result, he is ready to lead you through rally obedience courses, fetch your downed duck, or help you bring a smile to someone who needs a visit with a therapy dog. After your day is done, your fine, healthy Dachshund will sleep beside your bed, dreaming of your adventures the next day. Good nutrition is important to ensure that there will be many of those days.

BUILDING BLOCKS OF A BALANCED DIET

Eating right means taking in the materials we need to build and power our bodies. The same thing is true of your Dachshund. His species, his age, and his activities define his nutritional needs. This chapter gives you the basics you need and no fat or extra calories. Your Dachshund's food should provide the basic building blocks—a combination of proteins, carbohydrates, and fats, along with various vitamins and minerals—to live a healthy life.

One of our toughest jobs as consumers is understanding food labels. There are tricky bits in interpreting dog food labels, and many labels are misleading. Here you'll learn the principles you need to know so that you can select a high-quality diet for your Dachshund.

CARBOHYDRATES

Carbohydrates, stored energy from plants such as cereals and beans, have many jobs in your Dachshund's body. Some carbohydrates, like sugars, are absorbed directly into his bloodstream for quick energy—the pet equivalent of a "sugar rush." Other carbohydrates produce longer-lasting energy as they break down slowly in the intestine. Fiber, another kind of carbohydrate, contributes little nutritional value but helps the digestive tract work efficiently.

Your Dachshund's body uses protein to build muscle and perform other processes.

FATS

Fats, such as those from animals or plant seed oils, provide concentrated energy. Materials created from these fats make up much of the brain. In addition, these materials make up the fatty acids that work like delivery trucks, carrying vitamins through your Dachshund's body.

PROTEINS

Your Dachshund's body uses protein to build muscle, keep digestion and the nervous system working properly, and rebuild tissues as cells age and break down. Your Dachshund also needs protein to help convert other foodstuffs into glucose, a sugar that the body uses for energy.

Foods such as meat and beans contain lots of protein. When digesting one kind of protein, your dog's body harvests amino acids to use in building the many other different types of proteins he needs. His diet must provide the ten amino acids dogs cannot create through rearrangement of other amino acids. Think of cooking: Sometimes nothing other than a specific ingredient will do.

MINERALS

Minerals, found in the Earth's crust, collect in plants. When your Dachshund eats plants, usually in the form of vegetables in his diet, his body uses minerals, including calcium and phosphorus, to build blood cells, bones, and teeth. As with vitamins, some nutrients are essential in small amounts but become poisonous in excessive amounts. Calcium excess, for example, causes abnormal bone growth, especially in puppies.

VITAMINS

Vitamins, needed by living things for good health, must be taken in as food because the body cannot create them from other nutritional elements. Vitamins play an important part in almost every body process, so deficiencies can cause serious health problems, including vision problems, bone fractures, and an inability to fight off infections.

WATER

Water accounts for between 60 and 70 percent of an adult dog's body weight. Its nutritional role is to help regulate body temperature and enable food to move through the digestive system. Water is also a major component of the urine and feces that eliminate toxins and food waste from the body.

Inside the body's tissues, water is a major component of blood, which transports nutrients and oxygen to the cells. Water is also required for the chemical breakdown of food into energy and chemical components that form all the tissues in a Dachshund's body and govern all the processes that maintain him as a living being.

Furthermore, water provides lubrication for the joints and tissues, especially in the lungs, and forms the basis for the body fluids in which the chemical reactions that govern life take place. Water is a simple nutrient, but it is so important that a loss of 10 to 15 percent of the body's water content can result in death.

Fresh Water

Always make fresh water available to your Dachsie. Know that his need for water increases with exercise and may more than double in hot weather. Ideally, you should encourage your Dachshund to drink water during exercise.

Most dogs do well on tap water. However, if your dog does not like the taste of your water, try using filtered water to keep him hydrated. Dogs who are selective about their water can have digestive problems when their water is changed. If you suspect that this is the case, take bottles of your Dachsie's favorite home water with you when you travel.

WHAT TO FEED YOUR DACHSHUND

You want to feed your Dachshund a nutritionally complete diet that doesn't contain anything that will create problems for his body. Feed him something that he finds appetizing and that you find convenient to serve. Serve it in an amount that will maintain his body at an ideal weight. These are the basics.

Once you find a diet that works well, stick with that, as many dogs don't do well switching from diet to diet. Many first-time dog owners believe that their dog needs variety in his diet, and this idea is supported by advertising that shows a different gourmet dog meal for each night of the week. This is dog food formulated to appeal to the people purchasing it.

Experienced dog people will tell you that you can offer variety through treats, but that the basic diet your Dachshund needs should not be changed without a specific reason. Particularly during the transition to his new home and in times of family stress, your Dachshund's diet should be consistent. Puppies, especially, are still developing, and elderly dogs are usually set in their ways.

Unless your veterinarian directs otherwise, stick with the diet your Dachshund has been eating since he first arrived in your home. If you need to change his diet,

ask your veterinarian about the best ones that you can afford. Also, do not feed supplements unless your veterinarian suggests them—too much of a good thing can be harmful to your Dachshund.

COMMERCIAL FOODS

The most common commercial dog food types are dry, semi-moist, and canned. The moisture content of these foods ranges from 6 to 10 percent for dry, 15 to 30 percent for semi-moist, and 75 percent for canned. Most canned food has relatively more fat and protein and fewer carbohydrates than dry and semi-moist foods have and generally contains much higher levels of animal products.

Pet food labels must list the percentage of protein, fat, fiber, and water in the food. When reading labels, remember that what may appear to be a big difference in the amount of a nutrient—for example, 8 percent protein in a canned dog food versus 27 percent protein in a dry dog food—reflects the fact that there is more water in the canned food.

Once you find a diet that works well, stick to that, as most dogs don't do well switching from diet to diet.

Note: When comparing the nutrient value of wet food to dry food, the water content of the wet food changes everything. The higher the water content, the smaller the nutrient content, and the more food your dog must consume to get the nutritional value his body needs.

Dry Food

Dry food can help keep your dog's teeth healthy because chewing crunchy food helps reduce tartar buildup. Dry food grows bacteria if it becomes moist, so keep it in airtight containers once you've opened the bag.

Semi-Moist Food

Semi-moist foods come in a wide range of shapes, colors, and flavors. Generally the least nutritious of all dog foods, they contain many artificial ingredients. Perhaps useful as an occasional treat, they also include a variety of nutritional supplements and some dairy products.

Canned Food

Most dogs love canned—sometimes called "wet"— food because of its strong aroma. Feeding wet food mixed with the regular diet encourages old Dachshunds to eat. Wet food can also be a good option for Dachshunds with sensitive mouths. Dogs who regularly eat wet food need more dental attention because of the tendency of this food to stick to the teeth.

NONCOMMERCIAL FOODS

For most owners, creating your own dog diet is a poor choice; first-time owners especially should leave diets to the professionals. Although peoples' intentions are good in making their own diets, many have little knowledge. In addition, for all the fear created by the publicity over recalls of poor-quality foods, there is little publicity about the enormous amount of research that goes into nutrition for our canine companions by quality producers.

Most commercial diets that are made with whole ingredients (natural if not organic) are of higher quality than the diets that you can prepare at home. This is because dogs thrive on a consistently formulated diet. What is produced by the best commercial providers is high quality, comes in a variety of convenient forms, and will provide the nourishment your dog needs.

Homemade Diet

Homemade diets receive a boost each time there is a widely publicized pet food recall that undermines our confidence in the quality of ingredients used in pet foods. (This is why you should purchase the highest-quality dog food you can afford.) Some dog professionals and practitioners of holistic medicine prepare homemade diets for their pets.

Many people rave about the superior quality of their animals' health with these diets. However, the inconvenience and cost factors with this approach are significant. Selecting the ingredients and creating a diet that contains all the nutritional requirements for your dog, monitoring the calorie intake, and continuing to make the diet over months and years is a big commitment of time and money. If you purchase ingredients in bulk and freeze them, however, you can cut the cost of these human-quality food diets.

Homemade diets created from scratch should be made with the advice of a nutritionist or veterinarian. The complexities of calculating the percentage of calcium to phosphorous

Dog Tale

"Dachshunds will eat anything that doesn't eat them first—from bugs to French fries. Back 'in the day,' we didn't know how much harm we were doing feeding them from the table."
—Kathy Dorman, Dachshund owner

Homemade diets can be healthy, but they require a substantial personal commitment.

and fat to protein, for example, must be correct. In addition, you must calculate the relative amounts of vitamins and minerals contained in your homemade diet. Mistakes will directly impact your Dachshund's health. Therefore, the recipe formulation is best left to professionals.

Whole books are available on the subject of creating homemade diets. *The Whole Dog Journal* reviews commercially available "homemade" diets each year, which presents another alternative. Other recipes for home-prepared diets abound, but not all of them are nutritionally adequate. Rely on the advice of a veterinarian or veterinary nutritionist regarding your chosen recipes.

Raw Diet

The raw diets that first became popular among people who made their own dog food are now available in prepared packages, guaranteed to meet the nutrient profiles for "complete and balanced diets." Raw diets comprise fresh meat: ground muscle, organs, bones, fat, and connective tissues. Many are available at natural food stores or specialty pet stores.

Other diets, whether from a bag or a can, have been cooked in the creation or packaging process. The advantage of uncooked food is that heat-sensitive nutrients remain intact, requiring less supplementation in the diet. In addition, the ground raw bone that's included is an excellent source of calcium and other minerals.

The trouble that some veterinarians see in raw food diets is that without cooking, biological contaminants have not been eliminated. These contaminants, such as salmonella, are a hazard for the pet as well as for the handler of these foods. Counterarguments say that dogs have natural digestive fluids and enzymes that have evolved to deal with bacteria and other common pathogens; therefore, the contaminants pose no problem for the dogs.

Safe handling practices can protect human preparers of the food from any low-level bacteria normally removed by cooking. The handling issues are the same as those with meat intended for your table. Proper thawing and proper sanitation solve those problems, advocates say.

SUPPLEMENTS

If you are feeding a diet with complete nutrition, you should not feed supplements unless your veterinarian recommends them. Likewise, supplements in a diet should not pull you in the direction of that diet. Pick a diet with complete nutrition. Then, if your veterinarian suggests supplementation, do it. Some vets suggest supplementing with glucosamine and chondroitin for joint care in dogs with arthritis. Be aware that extra supplements may aggravate medical conditions, so always check with your veterinarian before giving your dog any herb or supplement.

TREATS

Treats can provide variety for your Dachshund's palate. Healthy treats include small pieces of carrot or apple, small amounts of peanut butter, and tiny pieces of rice cake. Alternatively, purchase low-calorie treats.

BONES

A large portion of the dog community feeds their dogs uncooked meaty raw bones. These marrow bones and joints provide quite a bit of chewing for your dog. However, these should be avoided because many veterinarians have a significant concern about dogs breaking

PUPPY POINTER

Offer your puppy his meal at the proper time. If he doesn't eat within ten minutes, pick it up. Otherwise, your adult dog will have you begging him to eat. Dachshunds are excellent person trainers.

Small pieces of apple (with the seeds removed) can make for healthy Dachshund treats.

teeth, swallowing parts of bones, and splintering bones, creating sharp edges that cut their way through the digestive tract; this terrible situation requires surgery to repair.

Some people suggest using rawhide bones instead, but these should never be given to your Dachsie, as they can be ingested and cause digestive blockages. Cooked bones pose a significant risk of splintering and should not be fed to dogs under any circumstances.

WHEN TO FEED YOUR DACHSHUND

Adult dogs do well fed twice each day, once in the morning and once in the late afternoon. Late-afternoon feeding gives your dog plenty of time to relax in the evening, have a walk before bedtime, and sleep through the night without getting hungry again.

Free feeding, or making food available all day, is a questionable practice for any dog. You get very little information about his appetite and energy level if he free feeds. Observing your dog's eating and drinking each day is a great way to monitor his health.

Dogs do not adapt well to frequently changing diets. If you have to change diets, mix the new diet with the old over a seven- to ten-day period, gradually increasing the percentage of the new diet. If you see increased stool bulk or looseness, the new diet may not suit your dog as well as the old one did.

OBESITY

Obesity in dogs is due to overfeeding and underexercising, complicates many diseases, and shortens your pet's life. Forty percent of US dogs are overweight, and many Dachshunds suffer from back problems aggravated by obesity. If you're not sure how to judge correct weight for your dog, use this guide: From above, you should see a waist-like effect after the last rib and before the hips. If you are unable to feel each rib, your dog is overweight.

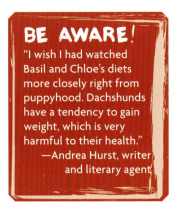

BE AWARE!

"I wish I had watched Basil and Chloe's diets more closely right from puppyhood. Dachshunds have a tendency to gain weight, which is very harmful to their health."
—Andrea Hurst, writer and literary agent

Discuss with your veterinarian whether you should simply feed less of the current food or feed something that is less dense in calories. Also, discuss the amount of exercise your dog should have, and increase physical activity slowly to allow your dog to come into condition.

Your veterinarian is your partner in determining a diet that works for your Dachshund. In general, she will advise you to avoid diets that contain additives, artificial coloring, and artificial flavoring. In addition, she can help you determine a healthy weight for your Dachshund. Know that you should not add supplements to a properly formulated commercial diet unless your veterinarian suggests that you do so.

CHAPTER 5

GROOMING YOUR DACHSHUND

Grooming can help strengthen your relationship with your Dachshund.

Grooming can be as extensive or as simple as you wish. If you are an older person with arthritis, you can keep your Longhaired or Wirehaired Dachshund's traditional look, but you'll need grooming help. If you love "doing hair," then you might put together a grooming station and do your Dachsie's "'do" up yourself.

Some Dachsie people don't mind performing simple brushing, combing, and bathing but prefer to leave clipping to the professionals. If you don't like grooming or taking your dog to a groomer, consider a Smooth Dachsie. However, even the Smooth Dachsie family should do some grooming because grooming isn't all about good looks.

WHY GROOMING IS IMPORTANT

Grooming is for your Dachshund what your grooming is for you—a way to feel clean, check your health, feel anchored by a routine, and increase your sense of well-being. Grooming is also a relationship reinforcer in the same way that brushing your child's hair is not just a matter of reestablishing an orderly appearance.

For all dogs, grooming not only keeps the coat mat- and tangle-free but also distributes natural coat lubricants and removes dirt and leaves, seeds, and burrs from his hair. In addition to keeping your Dachsie's coat in good condition, grooming is a chance for the two of you to spend time together each day in a relaxing situation.

GROOMING: THE SPA EXPERIENCE

From the second you call your Dachsie and lift him onto the table, grooming should be a pleasant experience, as a massage or spa day would be for you. Set up the grooming area for both you and your Dachsie's comfort so that you both look forward to grooming time. If your tools are laid out, the table is at the right height, the lighting is good, and a ready supply of treats is available, your Dachsie will be glad to lie still while you brush and care for him. Provide a reward for coming when called and for getting up and lying flat on the table.

Your tone of voice should be gentle. You can spend much of your time telling your Dachsie what a good and beautiful dog he is. He will not understand the words, but he will love being "fussed over." He'll hear the pleasure in your voice and will see the smile on your face. This is Dachsie heaven.

As you check your dog before you begin grooming, massage the spot right behind the ears and the spine right in front of the tail and gently smooth the hair on his face. This process of kind handling, relaxed talking, and petting helps build a positive relationship based on trust between you and your Dachsie.

Check on your Dachshund's health during each grooming session.

GROOMING AS A HEALTH CHECK

As you go about your grooming, start with the same foot each time. Have a look at the pads on your Dachsie's feet as well as his nails and dewclaws to ensure that they are in good condition. Groom between his toes to remove any mats or stickers.

As you part the hair and move upward, check for fleas and ticks and bumps or bruises. If your Dachsie seems to be tender in a spot or objects to being touched, move on and try again tomorrow, as long as there is no obvious injury. (If an area is persistently tender or sore, or extremely painful, take your Dachsie to the vet.) Check his eyes and ears and the area around his anus to be sure they are clean and that excess hair is removed.

Use the same pattern each time you groom so that your Dachsie becomes accustomed to the routine. While building trust through routine with Dachsie, you'll have done a health check and grooming in one step!

GROOMING STATION

If you're going to groom your Dachsie rather than taking him to a grooming parlor, consider setting aside a specific area for grooming where you can keep

Only use canine-formulated shampoo and conditioner for your dog.

your supplies and grooming table. An area that has running water, a bathing tub, and plenty of storage for towels and cleaning equipment, such as a Shop-Vac to clean up after grooming, makes the job pleasant. However, an elaborate setup is not necessary. Plenty of Dachsie people groom their dog in a bathroom or on a garage worktable.

GROOMING SUPPLIES

Depending on your ambitions, you'll need more or fewer supplies. Essential are a brush, a pair of scissors (to cut out any plant materials stuck in your Dachsie's coat), and bathing supplies, because nothing is as exciting as a roll in something that smells repulsive to people. A toothbrush is also needed.

A more thorough list of grooming supplies would include the following:

- **Bathing supplies:** These include a rubber bathing mat, gentle canine shampoo, oil-based canine conditioner, several large towels, a hair dryer, and anti-tangle spray for longer coats.
- **Brushing supplies:** You'll need a slicker brush (a wire claw–type brush) set into a base. This works well for thick coats but not on the body where hair is clipped short. The pin or bristle brush is suitable for clipped hair. The best combs are wide-toothed steel combs with wide-spaced pins at one end and closer-spaced pins at the other.
- **Dental supplies:** Your Dachsie will require a doggy toothbrush and canine-specific toothpaste or baking soda. (Mix 1 tablespoon [15 mL] of baking soda with 1 teaspoon [5 mL] of water.)
- **Ear care supplies:** These supplies include cotton balls, for placing inside the ears during bathing as well as cleaning the inside portion of the ear, and a mild alcohol-free cleansing solution.
- **Eye care supplies:** Along with some gauze or a soft cloth, you'll require a sterile veterinary eyewash.
- **Nail supplies:** You'll need a guillotine-style nail clipper and an emery board to keep the nails trimmed and smooth. Have flour or a styptic pen on hand to staunch bleeding in case you cut a nail too short.

- **Trimming supplies:** A pair of hairdressing scissors is an important tool. Scissors have to fit your hand properly and comfortably, as you'll want to purchase only one or two pairs in your Dachshund's lifetime. Finding a well-fitting pair of scissors is impossible without trying them. While some people prefer straight-bladed scissors, others prefer curved. This is a matter of individual preference. You might also want an electric clipper, for shaving longer coats, and a stripping tool for other tasks, including stripping your Wirehaired Dachsie's undercoat. Some breeders and groomers do this by hand, without a tool.

Smooth Dachshunds require less grooming than those with other coats.

COAT AND SKIN CARE

Your grooming session will differ depending on your Dachsie's coat and age. Puppy fur is different from adult fur; be prepared for your adult to lose his undercoat twice each year.

SMOOTH DACHSHUNDS

The Smooth Dachshund is by far the easiest to maintain. These sleek beauties require little more than weekly brushing with a soft-bristled brush (followed by a wipe with a cotton cloth), a nail clipping about once a month, and daily teeth cleaning.

Add some serious sheen to your Smooth

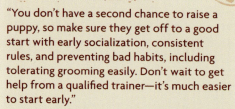

PUPPY POINTER

"You don't have a second chance to raise a puppy, so make sure they get off to a good start with early socialization, consistent rules, and preventing bad habits, including tolerating grooming easily. Don't wait to get help from a qualified trainer—it's much easier to start early."

—Kirsten Nielsen, PhD, Certified Pet Dog Trainer, Portland, OR

Dachshund's coat after brushing him by applying a drop or two of baby oil to your palms and smoothing the oil over his coat. By the way, some breeders use this secret: Keep shorthaired dogs looking good by running a stripping knife over their coats daily.

WIREHAIRED DACHSHUNDS

Wirehaired Dachshunds shed the least of the Dachshunds, but they require extensive grooming. They need brushing and combing at least three times a week, and every three months, they need to be stripped and bathed.

Stripping an undercoat seems mysterious until you learn that under their wiry hair, Wirehaired Dachsies have a soft undercoat that dies and sheds (as skin cells do). This dead hair must be removed (stripped) several times each year. You can do this yourself or hire a groomer.

The best advice is to talk with your breeder or long-time owners of Dachsies, look carefully at well-groomed Wirehaired Dachsies, and watch the process to learn how to strip them yourself. Basically, the process involves reaching under the topcoat and pulling out the dead hair. A stripping tool can be helpful; as mentioned, some groomers do this by hand, without a tool.

Alternatively, if you don't require your Dachsie's coat to be show quality, you can use an electric clipper to shave him regularly and keep the coat looking neat.

Wirehaired Dachshund coats require stripping several times each year.

LONGHAIRED DACHSHUNDS

Longhaired Dachshunds are beautiful, but they require a significant grooming commitment. They need daily brushing to get rid of the tangles and mats that seem to appear out of nowhere. Fortunately, most Longhaired Dachsies consider brushing to be the highlight of their day.

NEED HELP?

If you're having trouble getting your Dachshund to look as you imagined, pay a professional groomer to show you how it's done. (See section below: "How to Find a Professional Groomer.") Another great learning experience is to watch what happens behind the scenes at a dog show.

BRUSHING

Brushing not only keeps your dog looking good but is essential to the health of his skin and coat. Brushing distributes coat oils, stimulates blood flow to the skin, and removes dead hair that inhibits insulation. Brushing your dog every one or two days should also keep your home from becoming covered in hair during the spring and summer months.

Frequent attention helps keep your Longhaired Dachshund's coat clean and tangle-free.

Be careful to remove mats, especially in those places where your Dachsie's skin folds, such as under the legs and behind the ears. This is where rubbing causes tangles and mats his hair. When the hair mats, the amount of rubbing increases, causing skin tenderness.

HOW TO BRUSH YOUR DACHSHUND

Prepare and treat each grooming session like training. If your dog was not properly trained to accept grooming, you must be persistent and work in small steps. If you give up, you will encourage your dog to fight you.

Although some people prefer to brush their dog on the floor or on the couch in a favorite spot, grooming is easier for your back if you use a table where you can stand up straight. Some grooming tables allow you to leash your dog and hook him to an adjustable arm, but keep in mind that if you leave the table, your dog will likely follow, possibly resulting in a terrible accident. Even without a leash, jumping from the grooming table could severely harm your Dachsie, so never leave him unattended.

1. When you brush your dog, follow the direction of hair growth.
2. As with your own hair, brush a small section first, then comb.
3. If you find a tangle, use the brush again; grasp the hair between the tangle and the skin to keep the grooming from becoming painful. Keep in mind that using a spray detangler can help smooth out small snarls but won't fix a major mat.

Smooth Dachshund Notes

For the smooth coat, take care to use a soft bristle, a pin brush, or a comb. Start at the front of your dog and brush in the direction the hair grows. A rubber brush can work as well, or a grooming mitt. Clean around the eyes with a soft brush.

Wirehaired Dachshund Notes

Carefully brush twice a week with a wire-pinned brush to remove any tangles that may have formed. Start at the head and work backward. Once you have groomed the coat thoroughly, use the soft-bristled brush to remove any loose hairs. The face may need combing with a fine-toothed comb.

Clipping—shortening the hair using a battery-powered or electric device with blades, as in a barber shop—is a useful alternative to stripping or scissoring wirehaired coats. Blade size recommendations include #10 for the head, under the neck, and the ears and #5 (for clipped hair 1/2 inches [1.3 cm] long) or #7 (for clipped hair 1/4 inches [0.6 cm] long) for the neck, body, and tail. Scissor the eyebrows and beard to your preferred shape and length.

Always bathe your Dachshund in a warm environment so that he doesn't get too cold.

Before attempting clipping yourself, learn from a professional. Watch the process—not only the order of the grooming and the use of the blades but also the handling techniques. Some dogs are very compliant with clipping; others are not. The best breeders start handling and using clippers on their puppies to accustom them to this process.

Longhaired Dachshund Notes

As with your own hair, be sure to keep your Longhaired Dachsie's coat clean and tangle-free. Frequent attention, especially to areas where the skin meets (such as under the forelegs) and long hair strands twist together, helps keep your dog's coat in good condition. Brush, and if necessary, comb through the coat with a stripping blade to remove dead hair; finish by using a fine-toothed comb.

Untangle mats behind the ears by hand, using detangling spray when necessary. When finished with the body grooming, trim with scissors to create the classic "D" shape of the tail hair, the neat, finished look of the ears, and a smooth and even chest. Trim the excess hair on the bottom and front of the feet.

BATHING

Bathing allows you to clean Dachshund's hair and skin thoroughly, returning it to a pristine, natural condition. Be sure that you are bathing your Dachshund in a warm environment. In other words, if you wouldn't take a bath outside, don't consider that an alternative for your Dachshund. Remember, he's going to be wet for a while, and no dog, especially the very young or the very old, can withstand dampness and cold, especially if there is a breeze. In addition, you'll want to use slightly warm water.

Bathe your dog only occasionally—every 8 to 12 weeks. Choose a shampoo created especially for dogs; the pH of shampoo for canines and humans is different because the needs of their skin are different. With longer-haired Dachshunds, blow-dry on a low setting instead of allowing them to air-dry (after toweling dry), as you can with shorthaired Dachshunds.

HOW TO BATHE YOUR DACHSHUND

You'll learn from experience whether your Dachshund's coat requires that you groom out mats and tangles prior to wetting (using anti-tangle spray if needed) or whether the process works better if you detangle with your fingertips as you bathe. Your breeder can give you a guess about which way will be more efficient and comfortable for you and your Dachshund.

To bathe your dog:

1. Place a rubber mat in the bottom of the bathtub or sink to provide sure footing for your Dachsie.
2. Place cotton just inside both ears (his, not yours) to prevent water and shampoo from entering the ear canal. You may wish to wear a waterproof apron to keep your clothes dry.
3. Insist that your Dachsie stand still while being bathed. Although most Dachshunds enjoy a bath (and you want your buddy to enjoy himself), this is not playtime.
4. Wet his coat thoroughly with warm water. Start with the base of the body and work upward so that the water penetrates rather than runs off the coat.
5. Distribute the shampoo over his head, back, and torso and down his legs and tail and lather. Using a squirt bottle—like diner ketchup bottles—helps you control the amount

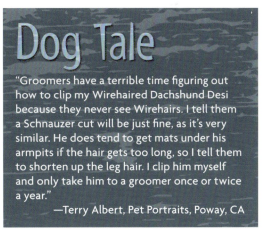

Dog Tale

"Groomers have a terrible time figuring out how to clip my Wirehaired Dachshund Desi because they never see Wirehairs. I tell them a Schnauzer cut will be just fine, as it's very similar. He does tend to get mats under his armpits if the hair gets too long, so I tell them to shorten up the leg hair. I clip him myself and only take him to a groomer once or twice a year."

—Terry Albert, Pet Portraits, Poway, CA

of shampoo and its distribution. You don't need too much shampoo, and an even distribution does a better job of cleaning.

6. Work the shampoo through the coat until you reach the skin. Be sure to bathe his underside, including his genitals, under his tail, and inside his earflaps.

7. Once your Dachsie's coat feels clean, rinse with warm water, starting from his head, using your hands to direct water and shampoo away from his eyes. Rinse his earflaps, neck, body, legs, and tail. Rinse underneath, ensuring that each layer of his coat is clean. Rinsing takes time. The saying is, "When you think you've rinsed enough, rinse five minutes more."

8. If your dog has a dry coat or skin, use an oil-based canine conditioner or add a teaspoon (5 mL) of coat oil to the conditioner. Massage in the conditioner and then rinse again. Double-check to ensure that your Dachsie's coat is squeaky clean before you begin drying.

9. Drying begins inside the tub with towels. Towel dry as well as you can. Then move your dog to the grooming table.

10. Turn on the dryer. Begin with the foot and move upward, brushing continuously until each section is dry before going on to the next. Brush each section until the hair is fluffy. When finishing, comb using the wide-toothed comb to ensure that tangles are removed. If you fail to brush and comb thoroughly when drying, your Dachshund's coat will mat.

DENTAL CARE

Dogs have the same dental hygiene issues that we humans do. When dogs' teeth are not attended to, bacteria and food particles form the yellowish substance plaque, which causes your dog's bad breath as well as potential tooth loss. Removing the food particles and the plaque is important to your dog's long-term health, as tooth loss also causes digestive and dietary challenges.

Not only do dogs find human

Ideally, you should brush your Dachshund's teeth once every day.

If you smell an ear odor, notice lots of ear scratching, or see the presence of ear mites, you must deal with it immediately.

toothpastes as distasteful as we might find their chicken-flavored toothpaste, but human toothpastes contain ingredients that are harmful if swallowed or inhaled. So use canine-specific toothpaste. Also select a toothbrush designed for a dog rather than for a human being. Dog toothbrushes are especially shaped for their mouths. Alternatively, brushes that slide over your fingers or a piece of gauze may be more acceptable to some dogs.

Ideally, you should brush your Dachshund's teeth once a day.

HOW TO BRUSH YOUR DACHSHUND'S TEETH

Start tooth brushing when your Dachshund is a puppy with healthy gums and teeth. Begin with gauze, a washcloth, or your finger in place of a toothbrush. Once your Dachshund becomes accustomed to this process, you can begin with the toothbrush. But there's no need to rush—go at your Dachsie's pace, and always praise him for cooperating.

Follow these steps to brush your Dachshund's teeth:

1. Gather your materials. You can use dog toothpaste or 1 tablespoon (15 mL) of baking soda with 1 teaspoon (5 mL) of water. As mentioned above, do *not* use toothpaste made for people.
2. If you use a grooming table, put him on the table. If not, use a well-lit utility area. Put your Dachshund in a *sit*. (To teach this cue, see Chapter 7.)
3. Apply the toothpaste and rub your Dachsie's teeth and gums gently in a

circular motion. Don't worry about cleaning the inside surfaces of the teeth because his tongue keeps these areas clean. The most important location is the outside surface where each tooth attaches to the gum.

4. Keep brushing sessions short and positive—30 to 60 seconds is enough. Then reward!

EAR CARE

For some Dachshunds, the hair growing inside their ears creates a damp, troublesome atmosphere. For this reason, many groomers and Dachshund owners pluck the hair from their dogs' ears using tweezers or their fingers. If hair plucking is necessary for your Dachsie, have an experienced groomer show you how to do this in a way that does not hurt.

Many long-time Dachshund people and some veterinarians believe, "The less you fiddle with a dog's ears, the better." A small amount of light brown wax in the ear is normal. However, some dogs have trouble with their ears. If you smell an odor, notice lots of ear scratching, or see the presence of mites—wiggling white specks on darkened dried blood spots—you must deal with it immediately. Proper care usually clears trouble within a few days.

HOW TO CLEAN YOUR DACHSHUND'S EARS

Have either your veterinarian or your breeder demonstrate ear cleaning to you before you try it yourself.

1. Clean the inside of the earflap gently with a cloth or gauze.
2. Clean the ear canal by applying a few drops of a mild alcohol-free cleansing solution, massaging the base of the ear to loosen secretions, and wiping out the visible portion of the ear with gauze or cotton balls. Never use cotton-tipped swabs in the ear canal, as this pushes debris further inside and commonly causes ear infections, and the swab might accidentally damage the ear canal.
3. Don't forget to provide a lovely treat to keep your Dachshund enthusiastic about ear cleaning.

BE AWARE!
Using a Dremel or grinding tool on nails can lead to trouble, especially with a longhaired dog. If the hair is caught by the Dremel, the twisting and pulling can be very painful. Don't take the chance. Clip your Dachsie's nails by hand and use an emery board to smooth the rough edges.

Dachshunds who have long hair on their nose and around the eyes often experience eye irritation.

EYE CARE

Dogs who have long hair on the nose and around the eyes often experience eye irritation from hair rubbing against the eyeball. In addition, pollen, dust, dirt, and other foreign material can provoke mucus and excessive watering.

Keep hair out of your dog's eyes, trimming perhaps much more often than you clip the rest of the body. At the same time, go ahead and wash the area in and around the eyes to remove any material that might be causing eye irritation. If the eye itself is red or the wetness comes from discharge rather than tears, take your Dachsie to the vet. Excessive wetness can be an indication of a health problem, such as allergies to dyes or food ingredients or a yeast infection.

HOW TO CARE FOR YOUR DACHSHUND'S EYES

1. Wash your hands and then put your Dachsie on a well-lighted table.
2. Carefully trim excess hair away from his eyes.
3. Clean the area around the eyes with a sterile veterinary eyewash. First tilt the muzzle up and steady the dropper against your dog's head. Squeeze the proper dose of drops into his eyes and gently work the wash in by moving the skin around the eye.
4. Use a moistened gauze pad or soft, lint-free cloth and wipe underneath the eye and gently blot and remove dried mucus.

5. Always provide a delicious treat to keep your Dachsie looking forward to eye care.

NAIL CARE

Dogs who regularly exercise on rough ground, roads, or concrete need less nail trimming than dogs who don't. But all Dachshunds' nails need to be trimmed regularly, perhaps once a month, to keep the toes in the proper position and to help prevent the nails from tearing and catching during normal day-to-day activities. Especially important are the dewclaws, if they have not been removed, because they can grow back into the pad and cause pain.

HOW TO TRIM YOUR DACHSHUND'S NAILS

Watch an experienced groomer before trying nail trimming yourself. Once you begin, move swiftly. Having someone help you restrain Dachshund or hand you things may be useful.

1. First, gather your materials together, including a guillotine-style nail clipper, an emery board, and flour or a styptic pen (coagulant) to stop the bleeding

Good professional groomers work efficiently while keeping your Dachshund comfortable.

quickly, in case you cut the nail too short. Be sure that you have adequate light to see the quick, the sensitive vein inside the nail, if your dog's nails are light colored. This will give you confidence that you're cutting nail and not skin or hair.

2. Put your Dachshund on the grooming table.
3. Take a foot in one hand, smooth the hair away from the nail, and put a finger under the toe.
4. Cut only the end of the nail, parallel to the toe pad. On white nails, avoiding the quick is easy. With proper light, you can see the vein inside the nail, dark with blood. On dark nails, you must simply clip only the very end of the nail because you won't be able to see the vein.
5. Once you've clipped all the nails, smooth each with an emery board to eliminate roughness.

HOW TO FIND A PROFESSIONAL GROOMER

A good groomer not only knows what the finished styling should be and can do the job efficiently, but she also manages the grooming process so that your Dachsie remains comfortable and calm. Begin researching potential groomers by asking your breeder, members of your local Dachshund club, and your veterinarian about good groomers in the area.

Next, visit the candidate groomers' shops. Observe the cleanliness of the facility and the demeanor of the pets being groomed. Ask about the bathing and finishing products your prospective groomer uses, and ask about the training and experience of the grooming staff. Inquire about cost. When you do select a groomer, leave a picture of the finish that you want. That way, your expectations are clear in advance.

If your Dachsie has problems with any part of the grooming process, let the groomer know. Likewise, question her about your Dachsie's behavior during his bath, blow-dry, clipping, and styling. If the groomer isn't good with your pet, look elsewhere.

HEALTH OF YOUR DACHSHUND

Annual veterinary exams help ensure your Dachshund's good health.

K eeping your best friend healthy requires some knowledge but mostly relies on close observation and a partnership with a veterinarian you trust. In this chapter, you'll learn about the common health issues for Dachshunds, some of which are related to their ancestry. But first, you'll learn how to find a veterinarian who will suit you and discover what happens at the annual veterinary exam.

FINDING A VET

When choosing your best friend's health care provider, look for a veterinarian who sees a lot of Dachshunds. If your breeder is nearby, ask which veterinarian she uses. In addition, your local Dachshund club will have a list of veterinarians with many Dachshund patients. Club members know the practice personalities, which makes your job easier. If you prefer holistic treatments, club members will know which vets use those techniques. Other resources for your search include the American Veterinary Medical Association (AVMA) (avma.org) and the American Animal Hospital Association (AAHA) (aahanet.org).

As with any professional service, you will have choices among location, quality of care, and cost. If possible, choose the veterinarian who sees more Dachshunds. Her familiarity with Dachshund-related problems will save you clinic visits.

ANNUAL VET VISIT

Properly nourished and exercised Dachshunds are likely to grow up healthy, but an annual examination is a good investment in your dog's health and emotional well-being. There is an art to getting the best from your annual exam. The first tip is to be prepared. When you call for the appointment, ask what you should bring. Usually, the list includes the following items:

• your dog's health records from your breeder
• the label from your dog's food
• a small, fresh stool sample
• your dog on a leash with treats and a favorite toy
• your list of questions

WHAT HAPPENS AT THE EXAM?

At your first annual exam, your veterinarian will observe and take information about your dog. While she is taking your Dachshund's history from you, your dog will relax, and she will observe his posture and movement and any signs of illness. She will take also Dachsie's pulse, listen to his heart and lungs to ensure that they are normal, and examine his body for fat deposits, tumors, and any indication of organ abnormality or parasites. Then she'll examine the legs and feet for their skin and nail condition. Finally, she will look with a lighted instrument inside your dog's mouth, eyes, and ears, checking for signs of abnormalities.

Based on the physical examination, your veterinarian may suggest diagnostic tests. At your first visit, expect a basic blood count so that she can have a normal result on file for future blood-test comparison. Your vet will also test the fresh feces you've brought with you.

VACCINATIONS

Part of each annual exam is to update vaccinations. Your Dachshund needs to be up to date on his adenovirus, distemper, parvovirus, and rabies vaccinations, which are considered core vaccines by the American Animal Hospital Association (AAHA). He may also need noncore vaccinations, such as Lyme disease, leptospirosis, and bordetella (kennel cough), given his age and lifestyle. Your veterinarian will discuss whether these are appropriate or necessary for your Dachshund. **Note:** Studies show that Dachshunds are at high risk for allergic and other adverse reactions to vaccines. Therefore, you should research nonessential vaccinations thoroughly before requesting them for your Dachshund.

ADENOVIRUS

Canine adenovirus is not a single virus, but a series of related viruses. Difficult to distinguish from other pathogens, adenovirus strains are not very common. They are spread through bodily fluids, especially urine, and are most likely to affect the liver, kidney, and eyes. Symptoms include yellowing of the eyes (or "jaundice"), an inflamed belly, vomiting, and pale feces. Treatment is limited to supportive care, including fluids to keep your dog's body properly nourished and his fluid contents balanced while the liver and kidney rest and recover.

PUPPY POINTER

"Teach puppies to use steps up and down from the couch and bed. Don't wait until after they've herniated their spinal disks as adults."
—Jill Kessler Miller, dog trainer, Los Angeles, CA

BORDETELLA (KENNEL COUGH)

Bordetella bronchiseptica, the bacterium that causes the contagious lung disease bordetella, spreads rapidly where dogs congregate: boarding kennels, dog shows, dog parks, grooming salons, and doggy day cares. Usually a mild disease, it is also called "kennel cough" because sufferers make a hacking cough. Bordetella is usually treated with antibiotics and cough suppressants; humidifiers can also ease symptoms. Although most adults recover in one to two weeks, Dachshund puppies who contract this disease require veterinary care to support their breathing and prevent pneumonia.

CORONAVIRUS

Coronavirus causes an intestinal infection that can be severe in puppies. Spread by contact with infected saliva and feces, depression and loss of appetite are followed by vomiting and foul-smelling orange diarrhea. Controlling vomiting and diarrhea and rehydration are the needed therapies. Vets recommend against coronavirus vaccination because the illness responds well to treatment.

DISTEMPER

Distemper is a highly contagious virus, spread through inhaling bodily secretions of infected animals. Distemper is most common in unvaccinated puppies from 6 to 12 weeks old because that's when the antibodies passed from the mother fall below protective levels. Sometimes mistaken for a cold, the disease causes symptoms including fever, loss of appetite, listlessness, and discharge from the eyes and nose. Later, secretions thicken and a dry cough and abdominal blisters develop. Vomiting and diarrhea become frequent. Two to three weeks later, seizures begin. If the dog recovers, neurological symptoms may persist. If you seek treatment early, distemper can be cured. To protect puppies, vaccinate for distemper by eight weeks of age.

LEPTOSPIROSIS

Leptospirosis is transmitted by the urine of infected animals through water or open sores. Most infections are mild, but they can cause vomiting, pain, and sometimes diarrhea or blood in the urine. Severe cases cause jaundice. Severely ill dogs need hospitalization, antibiotic treatment, and supportive care. Discuss with your veterinarian whether your dog needs vaccine, and if so, which variety is appropriate. Vaccine choices include those that protect against all four varieties of spirochetes and those that minimize the chance of allergic reactions to the vaccine. Continued protection requires revaccination every four to six months. Minis and Dachshund puppies have the highest chance of allergic reaction to the leptospirosis vaccine.

Bordetella and parainfluenza vaccines can be helpful for Dachshunds who frequent boarding kennels, grooming salons, and other places where dogs congregate.

Part of each annual exam is to update vaccinations.

PARVOVIRUS

Parvovirus is a highly contagious disease that attacks the gastrointestinal tract. Transmitted by contact with infected feces, the illness begins with depression, vomiting, and diarrhea. Some dogs develop fevers and severe abdominal pain. Dehydration occurs rapidly.

Dogs of all ages, especially puppies 6 to 20 weeks old, are susceptible. Suspect parvo in puppies who abruptly begin vomiting and having diarrhea. Recovery requires intensive veterinary care with hydration, antibiotics, plasma, and other supportive care for three to five days. Vaccination by eight weeks prevents most infections. All dogs should have a yearly booster and revaccination every three years.

RABIES

Vaccination is almost 100 percent effective against rabies, a fatal disease of mammals, including human beings. Transmitted through saliva in a bite, rabies has an aggressive form, where the animal attacks, and a form in which the animal staggers and stumbles. In either case, extensive drooling is a rabies symptom.

Assume dogs bitten by a wild animal were exposed. If your Dachsie has been vaccinated, revaccinate immediately and monitor at home for 45 days. If Dachsie has not been vaccinated, he must be checked for rabies immediately. Vaccines should be given as early as three to six months of age and then again every one to three years, depending on local and state laws. When traveling with Dachsie, take along proof of inoculation.

PARASITES

Parasites are organisms that live *on* or *in* your Dachshund, some of which can endanger your friend's life. Parasites plague most dogs during their lives. When your dog is stressed or ill, his immunity falters, the parasites reproduce, and infection becomes evident. Internal parasites live inside their host dog. External parasites live on the skin and hair of their host.

EXTERNAL PARASITES

External parasites aren't just uncomfortable—they can cause illnesses and spread disease. These parasites spread from one animal to another when a dog licks or sniffs another dog or encounters brush, grass, or feces where the parasite was deposited. Preventive measures can reduce the risk of your pet and your family catching external parasites.

Fleas

Fleas thrive in warm, humid conditions and can hop aboard your Dachsie in areas frequented by other animals. Signs of flea problems range from mild redness on a Dachsie's sensitive areas to severe scratching, which can lead to skin infections. An early sign is the appearance of black droppings on your pet's coat. You may not see the fleas themselves, but they can still be on your pet and in the environment. Depending on where you live, they may be a seasonal or year-round problem.

Fleas bite animals and suck their blood; young or small pets with heavy flea infestations may become anemic. Some pets can develop an allergy to flea saliva that may result in more severe irritation and scratching; these pets can become severely itchy from just one or two flea bites. In addition, tapeworms can infect a Dachsie if he ingests fleas carrying tapeworm eggs while biting at the flea irritation.

Treat your dog with a preventive during flea season. Always thoroughly clean his bed and crate. If he catches fleas, vacuum your floors and furniture to remove flea eggs, larvae, and pupae. With moderate or severe infestations, you may also need to treat your house and yard with an insecticide effective against fleas. Your veterinarian can recommend the appropriate flea control for your situation.

Mites

Dogs get ear mites through close contact with infested pets or bedding. Though tiny, ear mites can cause intense irritation that your Dachsie shows by shaking his head and scratching his ears. The scratching creates bleeding sores around the ears. Brown or black ear discharge is common with ear mite infections. Thorough ear cleaning and medication will eliminate the mites. Your veterinarian can show you how to clean your Dachsie's ears thoroughly.

Treat your Dachsie with a preventive recommended by your veterinarian during flea season.

Ringworm

Ringworm is a fungal infection seen on the face, ears, paws, or tail of a puppy or young adult. Spread easily between humans and pets through contact with infected hair (which can shed on furniture and carpets), ringworm causes symptoms including hair loss in circular patterns with scaly skin at the center. Treatments include antifungal ointment or shampoo (usually containing miconazole) or both.

Ticks

Tick exposure may be seasonal or year-round, depending on where you live. Ticks most often hop aboard a Dachsie while he's walking in the woods or in tall grass. After walks, examine his neck and ears, the folds between his legs and body, and between his toes. You can easily see or feel the ticks. Remove them by carefully using tweezers to grip the head as close to Dachsie's skin as possible. Gently and steadily pull the tick free. After removing the tick, you may drop it in a dish of alcohol to kill it and prevent contact with any of the fluid that carries disease.

Tick bites not only cause skin irritation but can also spread infections such as Lyme disease and Rocky Mountain spotted fever. Prompt removal lessens the chance of transmission. Consult your veterinarian about effective products and the proper schedule for preventive treatment. If your backyard breeds ticks, trim bushes and remove brush to reduce your risk of infestation.

INTERNAL PARASITES

Most internal parasites invade and live in the gastrointestinal tract. The most common exception is the heartworm. Installing a cement or gravel run for Dachsie to use for toileting (and cleaning and disinfecting it periodically) helps prevent worm infestations, especially in warmer areas of the country where parasites are difficult to control. Also, your Dachsie should take preventive agents. Remember, protection from internal parasites lasts only as long as you give the preventive medications.

Heartworms

Heartworms are a serious and widespread problem, most commonly along the Atlantic shoreline, the Gulf Coast, and major river systems. This is because mosquitoes spread heartworm disease. In heavy infestations, worms occupy the heart and its major vessels and the veins of the liver and lungs. Worms around the heart valves can interfere with the heart's pumping. Worms in the liver can

Check your Dachsie for fleas and ticks after he's been playing outside.

cause liver failure. Collapse and death can occur up to 30 days after treatment. In other words, even treatment is no guarantee that a dog can recover from a heavy infestation.

Early signs of heartworms include fatigue and a deep, soft cough. Dogs progressively lose weight, breathe more rapidly, and cough after exercise. For dogs with uncomplicated disease, the treatment protocol is to eliminate all adult worms and live young (microfilariae) and then use preventive measures. Drugs to eliminate the adult worms contain arsenic poison, and the elimination process is a physically exhausting risk for your dog. For critically ill dogs, surgery is an alternative way to remove adult worms.

Clearly, prevention is a superior approach. Dogs living in or visiting areas where heartworm is present must be on a heartworm prevention program. In areas where mosquitoes are a year-round problem, dogs should be on preventive drugs all year and for their entire lives.

Hookworms

Hookworms fasten onto the lining of the intestine and feed from the host dog. Most adult dogs ingest their larvae from the soil or through the skin. Dogs with chronic hookworm sometimes have no symptoms. When signs occur, you may see bloody diarrhea, weight loss, and progressive weakness. When dogs recover from hookworm, they still carry larvae in their tissues. Stress or illness can trigger their release, and then worms can reinfect the intestines.

Treatment includes a dewormer repeated at least once followed by testing to be sure that the parasites have been removed. Prevention includes good sanitation, periodic stool checks, and repeat deworming. Your veterinarian may recommend heartworm preventives that are also effective against hookworms and other worms. **Note:** Humans can contract hookworm.

Roundworms

Roundworms live in the stomach or intestines and can grow as long as 7 inches (18 cm). Adult dogs ingest their eggs from the soil or through an intermediary, such as a mouse. Although roundworms rarely cause symptoms in adults, young puppies can become very ill with heavy infestations, which are indicated by round bellies, dull coats, and stunted growth accompanied by abdominal pain, vomiting, and diarrhea.

Veterinarians can select a dewormer that suits the dog's age and health condition. Since most worm larvae form capsules around themselves (called "cysts") in various body tissues, they are protected from the dog's immune system

Roundworms require repeat treatments for thorough deworming.

Roundworms require repeat treatments for thorough deworming.

and the effects of most dewormers. Repeat treatments are necessary to kill worms that were in the larval stage during earlier deworming, and treatment must continue until the feces are free of worms and eggs. A preventive that targets heartworms and whipworms also thwarts roundworms.

Roundworms can cause serious illness in humans, especially young children who play in sandboxes. Preventing human infection hinges on recognizing that untreated nursing puppies are the source of most worm eggs. Frequent hand washing, especially after petting animals, and care about the cleanup of dog waste keep infection rates low.

Tapeworms

Whether as small as a grain of sand or as large as several feet (m) in length, tapeworms fasten onto the intestinal wall using their hooks and suckers. You may see their egg packets, like small, moving rice grains, near the anus. Although they drain nutrition from your Dachsie, tapeworms generally are not as serious as other varieties of worms.

Fleas or lice carry the most common kinds of tapeworms, so prevention of these external parasites helps prevent tapeworm infections. An alternative route of infection is through the eating of dead animals, which you control by confining your Dachsie to the yard and walking him on leash. Dewormers effective against

tapeworms are available from your veterinarian, along with guidance on how to use them.

Whipworms

Threadlike parasites that live in the intestines, whipworms grow 2 to 3 inches (5 to 7.5 cm) long and cause diarrhea and stools that contain mucus and blood. Your Dachsie's first symptoms may be urgency and straining during elimination. Heavy infestations cause weight loss and anemia. Three courses of dewormer treatment will eliminate whipworms. As with other worms' eggs, whipworm eggs remain in the environment for several years. To prevent reinfection, clean your yard daily and consider installing a concrete or gravel run. A combination worm preventive is effective against whipworms.

NEUTERING

Most Dachshund owners neuter (spay or castrate) their dogs for the control of unwanted puppies. Done before the first heat (or estrus) cycle, spaying reduces mammary tumors by 90 percent and prevents uterine cancers, cystic ovaries, false pregnancies, and other health problems. Contrary to myth, spaying does not change your female Dachshund's metabolism, personality, or instincts. The castration operation reduces a male dog's risk of prostate enlargement and tumors around the anus. Castrated males also tend to be less territorial and less likely to roam.

Although the traditional age for spaying or neutering has been about six months, the American Veterinary Medical Association (AVMA) guidelines allow dogs to be "fixed" as early as 8 to 12 weeks of age. Early neutering is often practiced at animal shelters. However, for Dachshunds who participate in sports, many vets suggest waiting until a puppy reaches adult size before neutering to provide extra joint protection.

BREED-SPECIFIC ILLNESSES

In the same way that characteristics for eye and coat color are inherited, Dachsie families inherit genes that are the basis of some diseases. Veterinary screening can tell you that puppies from a particular mating will not have genetic diseases. This is why you want your puppy screened before adoption. Although these checks don't eliminate the possibility that your dog will develop a health problem, you've done what is possible based on veterinary science.

CUSHING'S DISEASE

Of the three forms of Cushing's disease, most dogs have the pituitary-dependent (PD) form, a slow-growing cancer located in the pituitary gland that can spread.

The nonpituitary forms, found in dogs treated with cortisone, lead the body to misread the amount of cortisol it has. Symptoms include excessive appetite and thirst, frequent urination, a potbelly, hair loss, and drastic hair-texture change. Average life span with drug treatment is two years.

EPILEPSY (SEIZURES)

Some Dachshunds inherit idiopathic (or "primary") epilepsy, which causes seizures that are not the result of some other illness or trauma. Secondary epilepsy occurs as a result of chemical imbalances, exposure to poisons, head trauma, brain tumors, or infections, all of

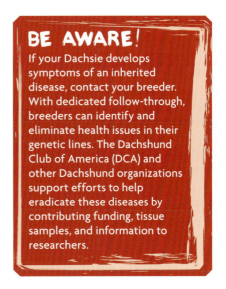

BE AWARE!
If your Dachsie develops symptoms of an inherited disease, contact your breeder. With dedicated follow-through, breeders can identify and eliminate health issues in their genetic lines. The Dachshund Club of America (DCA) and other Dachshund organizations support efforts to help eradicate these diseases by contributing funding, tissue samples, and information to researchers.

which cause uncoordinated firing of neurons. The prognosis varies depending on how early the disorder is diagnosed.

Mild seizures can pass quickly while a dog seems to look upward. Severe seizures can manifest as an unbalanced walk, aggressive or fearful behavior, or uncontrolled movement of limbs. Dogs may lose consciousness, paddle their limbs, and salivate, often losing control of their bladder and bowels. Vocalizations—described by owners as bloodcurdling screams—may follow.

Dachsie families inherit genes that are the basis of some diseases.

Decreasing the frequency and severity of the seizures is the treatment goal. Two-thirds of dogs with epilepsy can have their seizures controlled, although not without side effects of the drugs used to treat the condition. Common combination drug therapies include anticonvulsants, barbiturates, and antianxiety medications.

GASTRIC TORSION (BLOAT)

Bloat is an extremely painful condition that kills 25 percent of sufferers. With bloat, gas stretches the stomach to many times normal size. This causes tremendous pain when the stomach rotates, trapping gas inside and shutting down the blood supply to the heart and other organs. The result of swallowing air, bloat may have a genetic link.

To prevent bloat, feed multiple smaller meals each day instead of one large meal and reduce the speed at which your dog eats. (See "Food and Water Bowls" in Chapter 3.) Symptoms include unsuccessful attempts to vomit, pacing, and drooling. If you suspect bloat, get Dachsie to the vet immediately. If the stomach has not twisted, a stomach tube can release the gas. If twisting has occurred, a needle through the skin into the stomach releases gas. Surgery repositions the stomach and removes dead tissue.

HEMANGIOSARCOMA

Canine hemangiosarcoma results in incurable tumors of cells that line blood vessels. More common in dogs beyond middle age, this form of cancer develops slowly and is essentially painless, so diagnosis isn't usual until the advanced stages. Less than half of dogs treated with surgery and intensive chemotherapy survive more than six months. However, some studies show that up to 15 percent of dogs experience remission and extended survival.

INTERVERTEBRAL DISK DISEASE (IVDD)

Intervertebral disk disease (IVDD) causes the disks that cushion one vertebra from another to bulge or rupture. Bulging or rupture causes pressure or trauma to the spinal cord, followed by degeneration of the neurons involved in the spinal cord injury. A staggering gait is typical of minor damage, while more significant damage results in paralysis, especially of the hind legs. For many cases, surgery is the option. For mild cases, a conservative treatment of confinement and steroids may work.

Help prevent bloat by feeding smaller meals each day instead of one large meal.

KERATOCONJUNCTIVITIS SICCA (KCS)

When this condition occurs, a Dachsie experiences a dry cornea from lack of tear production; this lack of moisture can damage the cornea. Sometimes a mucus discharge accompanies the dry eye. The eye appears dull instead of bright. Necessary lifelong treatments include artificial tears and cyclosporine ointment.

PATELLAR LUXATION

When your dog's knee moves, the kneecap (or "patella") slides in a groove along the femur. With patellar luxation, the kneecap does not return to its proper position. This may result from injury or heredity and can affect either or both hind legs. Symptoms include difficulty in straightening the knee, limping, and twisting of the hock outward and toes inward. An experienced vet should screen your Dachsie puppy at six to eight weeks of age through manipulation of the kneecap. Treatment for this condition varies from medication for pain to surgery to repair ligaments.

GENERAL ILLNESSES AND INJURIES

Most dogs have one or more of these common illnesses and injuries in their lifetime. While upsetting, some can be well contained by catching symptoms and signs early; others can be prevented by thinking ahead.

ALLERGIES

Any dog can be affected by allergies, but they can also be inherited. Symptoms include intense itching, scratching, hives, and swollen eyelids. Antihistamines or medicated baths usually help. For flea allergies, eliminate fleas from the household and the dog, followed by monthly flea-control treatment for all pets. For inhaled allergies, wipe your Dachsie's coat to remove irritants. For food allergies, your veterinarian will suggest a limited-ingredient diet.

Dog Tale

"A friend's Dachshund had an odd smell. He learned that whenever he noticed that smell, his Dachsie's ears needed cleaning. He explained that long-eared dogs sometimes have problems with their ears. When I got my first Irish Setter, I knew what symptoms to watch out for, thanks to a Dachshund."
—Gail Parker, irishrescue.com, Philadelphia, PA

CANCER

Cancers are fast-growing tumors that invade tissues and spread through the

Call your veterinarian
if your Dachshund
shows signs of an ear
infection.

bloodstream. Resulting from mistakes in cell reproduction, they are linked to genetic causes. Signs include weight loss, vomiting, diarrhea, blood in the stool, and growths. Canine cancer treatments include removing tumors, radiation, chemotherapy, diet, and immune system therapies.

EAR INFECTIONS

Ear infections usually result from dampness or foreign material in the ear. Signs include head shaking, ear scratching, and tilting of the head. Dizziness and a bad odor coming from the ear can be signs of an inner ear infection. In addition, dogs often experience vomiting. Because this condition can affect your dog's hearing, you must see your vet. Cleaning and an antibiotic may be needed. Ask your groomer not to pluck your Dachsie's ear hair unless it is so thick that the canal remains wet—plucking causes waxy buildup, ideal for bacterial or yeast growth.

HEATSTROKE

Dogs depend on panting for cooling because they do not sweat (except for a small amount through their footpads). When the air temperature is close to their

HEALTH OF YOUR DACHSHUND

85

body temperature, panting does not work. Situations that commonly result in heatstroke are:

- confinement to a car, even when windows are open
- strenuous exercise in hot weather
- being muzzled while being dried with a blow-dryer
- confinement to concrete or asphalt without shade or fresh water

Symptoms of heatstroke include heavy panting, difficulty breathing, and sometimes vomiting and bloody diarrhea. Dogs suffering heatstroke may collapse, seize, and sometimes die. If you suspect heatstroke, get your Dachsie into an air-conditioned place and call your veterinarian.

If you are more than five to ten minutes from help, start rapidly cooling your dog by immersing him in cool (not cold) water for two minutes or until his rectal temperature falls below 103°F (39.5°C). At 103°F (39.5°C), stop cooling and dry. Rush him to the vet. Complications from heatstroke can occur hours or days later.

POISONING

Poisoning results from a curious Dachsie eating over-the-counter or prescription drugs, dead animals, rat poison, antifreeze, insecticides, or foods (such as chocolate and grapes) that are hazardous to dogs. If the source of the poison is obvious, pick up the container and take it with you to the telephone and then to the treatment center. If you're more than a few minutes from your veterinary clinic, call the ASPCA Animal Poison Control Center (open 365 days a year) at 888-426-4435. This fee-based call may save your Dachsie's life.

FIRST AID

First aid is doing what's necessary in order to safely transport your Dachsie to a medical professional. Remember, in an emergency, your first actions are to (1) keep Dachsie warm and calm, (2) stop the bleeding (if applicable), and (3) call your veterinarian.

First-aid materials recommended by the American Veterinary Medical Association (AVMA) include the following: **adhesive tape**, for securing or wrapping bandages; **a board, blanket, or floor mat**, which can help prevent further injury during transport; **phone**

BE AWARE!
"I wish I had known how easily a Dachshund can become paralyzed if proper precautions aren't exercised. When picking up a Dachshund, be careful that his back is fully supported, front and rear."
—Georganne Duron, adoptive Dachshund parent, Central Texas Dachshund Rescue

numbers for emergency services; **a gauze roll** (3 inches [7.5 cm] wide), useful for wrapping wounds or muzzling Dachsie in an emergency; **medical records** with medication and vaccination history, to assist emergency personnel in determining treatments; **milk of magnesia and activated charcoal**, to absorb poison (but only when directed by your vet); **nonstick bandages and towels**, to control bleeding or protect wounds; **a large syringe**, for oral treatments or to flush wounds; and **a digital fever thermometer**, to check Dachsie's temperature rectally.

During weekends, holidays, and evenings (times when most veterinary practices are closed), you will need access to a "Dachshund emergency room." Once the emergency occurs, you won't have time to shop. Ask your veterinarian for the after-hours treatment center she recommends for Dachshunds in her care and keep that center's telephone number, address, and directions posted in an easily accessible place. If you are traveling, consult the Veterinary Emergency and Critical Care Society (veccs.org) for a searchable list of emergency clinics by state.

ALTERNATIVE THERAPIES

According to the American Holistic Veterinary Medical Association (AHVMA), the holistic approach is to examine various aspects of your dog's situation (including his environment, disease pattern, and relationship with you) and combine conventional and alternative therapies to treat disease. Holistic practitioners believe that the challenge lies in learning the true root of the illness. Simple-appearing symptoms may have several layers of cause, and only when those causes have been found can there be lasting recovery.

ACUPUNCTURE

Veterinary acupuncture aims to strengthen the body's immune system, relieve pain, and improve organ function. Using ancient Chinese methods as well as modern electrodiagnostic instruments, acupuncture stimulates points on the body associated with energy paths. A common veterinary use of acupuncture is easing arthritis pain.

CHIROPRACTIC

The AHVMA describes chiropractic therapy as addressing a broad spectrum of conditions by identifying a fixated vertebra in a patient's spinal column and making specific adjustments that can relieve various problems.

HERBAL MEDICINE

Herbal medicine uses plants and their extracts to treat disease and maintain health. Western, Ayurvedic, and Chinese herbs balance "emotional, mental, and

Holistic practitioners develop treatment plans based on comprehensive research of your Dachshund's life.

physical dimensions," according to the AHVMA. Herbalists believe that whole plants provide a broad spectrum of desirable effects that allows practitioners to strengthen chronically ill patients.

HOMEOPATHY

Homeopathic remedies are often made from plants and minerals. Generally, when people speak of homeopathic treatments, they refer to remedies used for the relief of symptoms. In addition to the remedies made from plants and other essences, homeopathy also includes heat, moisture, massage, and other sorts of noninvasive methods to relieve the effects of illness.

PHYSICAL THERAPY

Physical therapy includes many methods of treatment, such as therapeutic ultrasound, exercises, hydrotherapy, massage, heat and cold therapy, and low-level laser therapy. These treatments can help reduce inflammation, aid in the repair of tissues, strengthen muscles, relieve pain, and restore movement. TTouch, a physical therapy method developed by Linda Tellington-Jones, is described by the Tellington TTouch Training website as intended "to activate the function of the cells and awaken cellular intelligence—a little like 'turning on the electric lights of the body.'"

SENIOR DOGS

At age eight or nine, Dachshunds enter their senior years. Well-cared-for Dachsies usually live to be 14 to 16, and senior dogs, like senior people, need special treatment as they age. Careful observation of your Dachsie's behavior will provide clues about the changes in his body. Common adjustments needed include food texture, number of calories, dental care, and understanding and tolerance for his mood.

KEEPING YOUR SENIOR HEALTHY

Find a high-quality food for seniors with smaller, softer pieces and less protein so that meals are easier to chew and digest. Reduce calories as your Dachsie becomes less active. Excess weight increases his risk of severe back injury. Take him for a walk at least once a day to keep him trim, reduce arthritis pain, and guard against heart disease and diabetes. Provide chew toys to improve his dental health.

Old dogs lose muscle mass and fat, causing them to get cold easily. Provide a thick, soft blanket and a warm place for your Dachsie's bed, as well as a coat for winter walks. Because an older dog's skin gets drier with age, reduce bathing frequency to prevent skin flaking and itching. Instead, massage your dog using a cloth. Gentle massage relaxes the muscles, feels good, and reassures.

OTHER ACCOMMODATIONS

Some changes in your Dachsie may be disturbing for you. His sight, hearing, taste, touch, and smell will dull, and his reaction to your call or a scampering squirrel may slow. He may also have mental and behavioral changes, such as impatience with anything that disturbs his sleep or children's urging to play. Often, older dogs may react by nipping. Protect your Dachsie's peace by separating him from children or household guests, and just let him relax.

A common and frustrating problem is inappropriate elimination; your once well-behaved pet may have trouble controlling his bathroom habits. If you are away all day, he may simply not be able to control his urine or feces. Plan accordingly. Set up an exercise pen indoors and line the bottom with plastic. Senior dogs have earned this extra care.

TRAINING YOUR DACHSHUND

Training is life-changing, but like most worthwhile pursuits, it doesn't happen overnight. If you want results, you must develop the habit of training. Training isn't simply a "session" at a given time each afternoon, although teaching new behaviors can be that. Training takes place all day, every day, as you reward behavior you want and avoid rewarding behavior you don't want.

A key to training success is to make it fun, to integrate training into every aspect of your life with Dachsie, and to have reasonable expectations of yourself and of your dog. After all, you're not a professional dog trainer. However, your Dachsie is a professional person trainer, so you need some training skills. That's what this chapter is about—showing you why and how to teach your dog the meaning of some basic commands.

WHY TRAIN YOUR DACHSHUND?

You've probably met people whose dogs jump on you and bark. Admit it—you're relieved when they hurry past you, too busy to stop. Not only is a well-trained dog allowed in more places, but you are happy to take a well-behaved Dachsie everywhere with you.

In addition to teaching your Dachsie what you expect, training helps you learn to communicate clearly. You can walk, have quiet times, groom, travel, meet new people, and celebrate, all with clear expectations of one another. Besides, Dachshund people warn that when you're not training your Dachsie, he is training you.

WHY POSITIVE TRAINING IS IMPORTANT

A woman meets a friend on the street. The friend's child has an ice cream cone. We all know what's going to happen, yet the woman ignores her dog. Then, when dog lunges for the ice cream, she says, "No, don't do that. Bad dog." She blames the dog for bad behavior.

Here's a better way to handle the situation, featuring you and your Dachsie. The toddler waves the cone at your Dachsie. "Down. Stay," you say, and your dog lies at your feet, your body positioned between him and the toddler. The toddler's ice cream ends up on the street, as predicted, but your Dachsie ignores it.

Your Dachsie has behaved well because you told him what to do. ("Down. Stay.") You didn't wait for trouble and then say, "No." There are exceptions, but generally speaking, "No" is not very helpful—when you say, "No," your dog doesn't know what he *should* do. Positive training tells him what to do.

MORE ABOUT POSITIVE TRAINING

Asking for and rewarding what you want is the secret to good training. Your Dachsie learns *down–stay* because you help him understand what to do when you make that sound. You guide him, using a combination of lures or inducements, making it easy for him to do what you want, and reward the behavior.

Positive training doesn't rely on electronic collars or rolling dogs over to show them who's boss. Positive training doesn't include yelling, pushing, shoving, or spanking. Positive training is about your dog willingly performing a behavior, with your praise or treats as reward. Dachshunds are terribly smart, stubborn, and sometimes deliberately naughty. Punishment will never help you get what you want from your Dachshund.

PUPPY POINTER

"Playful" exactly describes both the voice you should use to praise and give commands to your Dachsie and the voice to which he'll respond best. Puppies, in particular, are sensitive to harsh voices. Keep that happy voice, even when you are frustrated. If you're not happy with your training results, find help.

SOCIALIZATION

Socialization is the gradual exposure of your Dachsie to aspects of his new life, including sights, sounds, smells, other dogs, children, and new people. A well-socialized dog fits into his environment well because he is accustomed to both the regular and occasional features of life.

HOW TO SOCIALIZE

If your breeder has done a good job in the first eight weeks of your Dachsie's life, he already knows about radio or television programs, visitors, and children. He has been exposed to a wide variety of toys and different types of surfaces, climbing over and under things with his littermates. As he moves into your home, he'll learn about the new neighborhood, your family members, and neighbors.

Although Dachshunds are known for their courage, you can overwhelm and frighten a new pet without intending to. Gradually introduce new people and places, sights and sounds, so that your Dachsie is not overwhelmed experiencing them all at once. Provide treats to reward acceptance. When he sits in the presence of something new, treat. As your Dachsie gains confidence, treat him for going closer.

After your new dog feels more comfortable around new people, you and your friends can entertain him by playing with a ball and other toys. You can take short walks in your yard or enjoy short adventures in the car. Your dog can get out and meet people, hear new sounds, see new sights, and smell the flowers. A well-socialized dog is comfortable in most situations.

Positive training is about your dog willingly performing a behavior, with your praise or treats as reward.

CRATE TRAINING

Many first-time dog owners misunderstand the use of the crate and fall prey to the feeling that crates are jails and that using crates is cruel; the opposite is true. Properly introduced and used, crates become safe havens and places of peace and quiet. How does this happen? Because the mother dog feeds her puppies in a den, dens are places dogs associate with warmth and safety and seek throughout their lives. Your job is to ensure that this natural association continues.

In the modern home, the crate is a den. For this reason, you must never use the crate for punishment, and you must never allow children or any other pet to use it. Ensure that your Dachsie does not need to defend his crate, because it is his safe place.

View your Dachsie's crate as a tool that allows him to travel more places and be more a part of family life than a dog who is not crate trained. Crates are safe places when he cannot be supervised. They separate him from dangerous household items, some visitors—including fragile adults or children afraid of dogs—and household activities that might be hazardous, such as cleaning the house or removing hot food from the oven. Crates also assist in housetraining and in preventing household disasters, such as Dachsie bolting through open doors, especially during the holidays or family parties.

HOW TO CRATE TRAIN

To make the process of crate training easier, many experienced trainers borrow several crates and position them where their dogs spend lots of time. That way, there's a place to secure your dog quickly when you need to pay attention to something else. (This is temporary.) Line each crate with a soft towel and keep their doors fastened open so that they won't hit and frighten your "trainee." Make being in the crate special by providing a favorite toy or two to enjoy only when he's inside the enclosure.

Once your crates are ready, begin crate training your Dachsie by (a) practicing confining him in the crate, (b) feeding him meals in the crate, and (c) having him sleep in the crate. Each time you put your dog into the crate, follow the same steps:

1. Say, "Crate," as you toss a treat far inside so that Dachsie must get in to eat it.
2. When he enters, say, "Yes." Sound excited about Dachsie going into the enclosure.
3. Give him a chew and a favorite toy to keep him occupied and close the door quietly.
4. When you return to the room, say, "Good dog." Give Dachsie a treat and then release him.

Note: If Dachsie whines (except at night when he hasn't gone potty recently), wait until he is quiet to release him from the crate. Otherwise, you'll train him to whine when he wants to leave the crate. Especially while you're housetraining, take him to his potty spot when you release him from the crate.

A) Crate Practice

Practice confining your Dachsie for short periods while you're home so that crating does not always mean he is being left alone. Then you'll be able to crate him without too much resistance when you leave. Use a treat and your chosen command, either "crate" or "kennel." (Make sure everyone in the household uses the same command.) Sit near the crate for a while after he has gone inside and then go out of sight. Return and sit nearby for a little while. Then release your dog from the crate. Gradually increase his time in the crate and boost the number of sessions to several times each day.

B) Feeding Meals in the Crate

Place your Dachsie's food dish all the way back in the crate. If he is reluctant to eat entirely in the crate, place the dish as far in as he will go freely. Move the dish back each day. Once he is eating comfortably, close the door while he eats and open the door as soon as he is finished. With each feeding, leave the door closed for a few more minutes.

When you take your puppy or adult-in-training out of the crate, take him directly outside and let him potty. Then play for a while. Your Dachsie should remain quietly in his crate for up to 30 minutes after he eats. Longer than that

risks an accident. And playing after potty reminds him that remaining quietly in the crate comes with a big reward at the end.

C) Sleeping in the Crate

Keep a crate in your bedroom so that your Dachsie is not socially isolated at night. Put him in the crate using the command you choose (like "crate" or "kennel") and a treat. Remember, puppies need to go outside during the night, and you want to hear your puppy when he whines to let you know that he needs to go potty.

THE WORKING DOG OWNER

Adult dogs can tolerate crating up to eight hours, but if you are a working person with a dog who chews unless supervised, consider two alternatives. First, consider doggy day care at least several days each week. Alternatively, or in addition, dog-walking services will take your crated Dachsie out for a stroll, a potty, and some playtime about halfway through your workday. Although dogs sleep quite a bit during the day, what you don't want to do is create the problem that your Dachsie is unhappy going into his crate because he's left there too long. His crate should be a refuge, a place he goes willingly.

TRAINING YOUR DACHSHUND

HOUSETRAINING

A housetrained dog knows how to ask to go outside to his potty place. He also knows he should wait until you arrive home before he goes potty. Housetraining itself can be simple. All you have to do is create a potty schedule and stick to it, keeping three things in mind: (1) making clear to Dachsie where his potty place is, (2) the frequency with which new and anxious dogs may need to potty (usually every hour at first), and (3) signs that Dachsie is asking to go outside.

THE HOUSETRAINING SCHEDULE

Create a housetraining schedule that includes potty trips after every meal, whenever you return home throughout the day, and according to the frequency that your Dachshund will have to potty according to his age. Whatever you do, stick to the schedule. Set your phone to chime as a reminder. Otherwise, your Dachsie may have been pacing and whining while you were on the phone or answering e-mail. Ignored, he will pee because you are not paying attention.

Each night, pick up your Dachsie's water bowl about 30 minutes before his bedtime. Because a dog will not normally potty where he sleeps, crating him before bedtime reduces the chances of overnight accidents. Just before crating, take him to the potty place. Depending on his age, set your alarm to wake you up whenever you need to take him out, which may be multiple times each night. Repeat to yourself, "This will be worth it."

POTTY PLACE

Dogs need to eliminate anytime anything goes into their stomach. When your Dachsie drinks substantial amounts of water, he will also soon need to go potty. Throughout the day, your Dachsie will nap, play with his toys, and drink water, all of which will also make him want to potty. Watch him closely whenever these things happen, and bring him to the same spot outside when he shows signs of needing to potty. This is his potty place. When he asks to go outside, don't wait. Otherwise, he'll learn that you ignore his requests to go outside and will stop making them. Worse, he may hide his potty mistakes until you find them hours or days later.

POTTY FREQUENCY

Behaviorist Dr. Sophia Yin, author of *How to Behave So Your Dog Behaves*, says that a dog's age in months approximately equals the hours between potty breaks. So for example, if he's two months old, he can wait two hours to eliminate. (However, it's unreasonable to expect even an adult dog to wait more than eight hours after his last potty break.) In general, you'll repeat the potty/reward cycle six to eight times each day. Some puppies need hourly potty trips. Now you know why some people adopt older dogs.

POTTY SIGNS

Signs that Dachsie needs to potty are sniffing, whining, panting, circling, or wandering. When you see a sign of restlessness, such as an anxious look or squatting as he begins to potty, clip on the leash and power walk Dachsie to the potty place. No dawdling. If he doesn't pee and poop, pop him back into his crate for 15 minutes and try again. Repeat until he's peed and pooped, or he'll potty in the house as soon as you're distracted.

TRAINING THE POTTY COMMAND

1. When you take your Dachsie for a potty break, leash him and power walk him to the designated spot. Stand silent, neither petting nor distracting him until he has both peed and pooped.
2. As he's about to potty, say, "Potty," once so that he associates the word with the action.
3. Reward him as he finishes with a treat. Additional rewards include a quick play session or a short leash walk.

INTERRUPTING AN INDOOR EVENT

When your Dachsie begins to pee or poop indoors, give a sharp, "Aaah aaah!" which will stop the flow. Pick him up and carry him to his potty spot. This process of interruption teaches your Dachsie that *indoors is not okay*. Don't punish or frighten him, or he'll hide from you the next time he needs to potty indoors. Just the sound and taking him to his potty place accomplishes the purpose. No discipline is needed.

If your Dachsie has an indoor incident, clean thoroughly with soap and water and then use an enzyme cleaner to remove the smell. If the accident closely follows a successful potty trip or he's drinking excessive amounts of water, call your veterinarian. He may have worms or another intestinal problem that causes this behavior.

Sticking to a schedule is the surest way to avoid "accidents." Keep in mind that as hounds, Dachshunds do not consider cleanliness their top priority—your attention is—and their stubborn streak leads to mischief. One act of Dachsie defiance and mischief is to potty where they know perfectly well they are not allowed, gaining your full attention.

BASIC COMMANDS

These commands are the ones that count. When you create a solid foundation for your dog's training with these basics, everything else is easy. However, without your Dachsie knowing and respecting these basics, you cannot go further in your training relationship.

Come, *sit*, *down*, *stay*, and your release word are commands you should practice all the time. Don't forget to reward your dog periodically with an extra scratch and always a warm "good" when you get the response that you need. When you use that loving tone in your voice in response to your dog's compliance, your dog will work hard for you.

RELEASE WORD

For every command, there is the sound the dog hears that has a specific meaning, such as "sit," or "come," or "down," and there is a second sound that means, "You're free to do what you want. The command is over." This second sound is the release word.

The release word should be a word that is not in your common vocabulary. "Free," "release," "all done," and "zebra" are examples of good release words. Poor words are "okay" and "good." "Okay" is said many times each day in normal conversation, confusing your dog, while "good" is a word that you use to praise your dog.

Choose one release word to use with your Dachsie, and stick to it. He will be waiting to hear that word, which means that he is free to do what he chooses. That is music to a Dachsie's ears.

How to Teach a Release Word

You can practice this with breakfast each morning, with your games, and with any activity that you do with your Dachsie. You need a reward, preferably a high-value treat to start, and he needs to know at least one other basic command.

Start with your dog on the leash. This gives him the notion that you're working together. This also gives you a way to easily reposition him.

1. With your dog on the leash and a treat in your hand, say, "Sit."
2. Quickly say, "All done."
3. Allow your dog to walk forward to get the treat.

As you repeat, increase the time between the command, such as *sit*, and the release word, when your dog is rewarded. Practice this several times each day. When your dog rises before you give the release word, simply restart the process. Don't give him praise or a treat unless he stays sitting until the release word. Your Dachsie will get the idea quickly.

Keep the interval short, not confusing your dog with additional intervening commands or talking, and always do this on the leash, perhaps after some

TRAINING YOUR DACHSHUND

exercise. In other words, help your dog be successful. Don't start with college-level expectations when you have a preschooler.

SIT

When you need your Dachsie to stop what he's doing, one simple way is to have him do something else. The perfect command for this is *sit*. Also, the sitting position is one from which your Dachsie can start to respond to other commands, such as *down*. The command *sit* means, "Move to the sitting position from wherever you are now."

The act of sitting is also a way for your dog to ask your permission to do something. You will require your Dachsie to sit before you give him dinner or a favored toy, before he crosses the doorway into the next room, and before he greets guests. In other words, *sit* is a prelude to anything that's fun. Used by many trainers, "seeking permission" creates a positive basis of working with your dog. This habit is especially important with breeds that can be somewhat difficult to train, like Dachsies can be.

How to Teach *Sit*

1. Hold a treat just above your Dachsie's head. When reaching for the tidbit, his head will go up and his bottom will go down.
2. Say, "Sit." **Note:** When you're teaching the command, say the command *as* you get the behavior. Otherwise, your Dachsie won't associate the sound of the word with the action you want.
3. Repeat several times each day. Rapidly, you will be able to use "sit" to ask for your Dachsie's position.

One important note is to say any command only once. When Dachsie has learned the command, and, for example, you have asked for him to sit, do nothing until he sits. If he does not sit down, look away and wait. When he sits, give lots of praise. Then use your release word: "all done," or "free," or "zebra."

Dog Tale

One Dachsie owner related, "My Dachsie was pawing at me on his *sit*. A trainer advised that I release my Dachsie more quickly. In other words, I created the pawing by allowing my Dachsie to become bored. Change pace often and train only after your Dachsie has had plenty of exercise. The goal is to reward wanted behavior and to avoid creating behavior you don't want."

Dogs must come
when called so that
you can keep them
from danger.

COME

Dogs must come when called so that you can keep them from danger or interrupt destructive behavior. If your Dachsie sneaks out the front door and scampers toward a busy street, you want him to return to you when you call. If your Dachsie is chewing a pill bottle, rather than saying, "Stop that," say, "Dachsie, come." Your Dachsie will stop what he is doing and come.

Dogs don't understand the concept of stopping what they're doing because they're doing a lot of things at once—they don't know which thing you want them to stop doing. However, dogs do understand *come*. Give this positive command and your Dachsie will come to you so that you can supervise him or remove him from a dangerous situation.

How to Teach *Come*

1. Start training *come* from a close distance, perhaps inside the exercise pen or at the end of the leash. You can be very interesting if you kneel or sit down and clap your hands.
2. Use a happy voice to say, "Dachsie, come." When your Dachsie comes, say, "Yes," and give a treat.
3. Continue practicing this command in various secure situations, such as outside after a potty stop, with your Dachsie on the leash.

TRAINING YOUR DACHSHUND

103

The key to success with training, especially with a "sometimes-stubborn breed" such as the Dachshund, is to provide treats and praise as rewards and to create situations in which your dog will be successful. If you turn your Dachsie loose in a field with rabbits and call him, you'll have no success. If you put him on a leash to start and work up to "off leash in the house," he will learn to succeed and your relationship will become stronger as a result.

Many trainers suggest that you tether your new dog to your waist with a hands-free leash to reinforce his following you. This habit also allows you to call your Dachsie and know that he will follow you. Once he learns proper behavior, you can allow more freedom. People new to dogs often become frustrated that their pets don't behave well, but good behavior comes from patient teaching.

STAY

Stay means, "Wherever you are, whatever you're doing, stay motionless until I tell you to do something else." Use this command to keep your Dachsie on his rug during the family dinner or while you clean up a shattered glass. Difficult to teach because it is not associated with any one action your Dachsie should take, you must train and reward *stay* throughout your life together.

How to Teach *Stay*

1. Begin with your Dachsie leashed and seated on your left side.
2. Holding the end of the leash in your left hand, sweep the flat of your right palm toward your dog, ending in front of his nose. Say, "Stay."
3. Step one foot back. Let a second pass. Say, "Yes," to mark the behavior you want.
4. Give your release word. Treat.

After three repetitions, play a short game or toss a ball for your Dachsie to retrieve. Then practice again. Variously step to the right and then forward while your Dachsie stays for five seconds, then ten. Practice this command, increasing the time between the word "stay" and your release until you reach two minutes.

You can practice *stay* each time you feed your Dachsie. Before filling his bowl, pick up his meal with your right hand, say, "Stay," and place the empty dish on the floor. When your Dachsie dives for the dish, pick it up. Treat your dog for the time that he's staying. Repeat until your Dachsie holds his position when you put the dish down. Then say, "Yes." Give your release word and pour the meal into the bowl. Having been released, your Dachsie can eat. After several meals, he will have this command in his vocabulary.

For Dachsies who require grooming on a table, use the occasion to teach *stay*. Starting as young as eight weeks, place your Dachsie on a grooming table in a corner so that there's a protective wall on two sides. Say, "Dachsie, stay." Standing close, brush your Dachsie. If he comes toward the edge, put him back and repeat, "Stay." When you've finished brushing, give your release word and treat him with an excellent meaty treat.

DOWN

Down, which signifies your Dachsie lying down, is useful when you want your dog to relax. You can use *down* as the first step in a trick or put your Dachsie in a *down* in his crate or exercise pen while you remove his leash. You can also ask for *down* just because the grass is lovely and your Dachsie will love the cool on his belly.

How to Teach *Down*

1. The easiest way to teach *down* is to start with your Dachsie leashed and in a *sit*.
2. As you say, "Down," lure him into the *down* position with the treat between the fingers of your free hand.
3. Mark the position you want by saying, "Yes."
4. Allow your Dachsie to eat the treat.
5. Use your release word.

Your Dachsie should learn to walk nicely on a leash so that your life together is pleasant.

HEEL (WALK NICELY ON A LEASH)

Your Dachsie should learn to walk nicely on a leash so that your life together is pleasant. Even if you have a bad back, you should be able to walk your Dachsie comfortably. In addition, your Dachsie should walk nicely on a leash for anyone, not just you. This gives him the basis for a flexible life. Your friends can walk your Dachsie. He can have a dog walker at lunchtime if you're not at home. Good manners make your dog's life richer.

Heel means, "Walk with your shoulder by my left knee." This is the command you use when you walk Dachsie in your training sessions, and this same position is how Dachsie should walk on a loose leash on your neighborhood rambles. With an untrained Dachshund, what usually starts out as, well, walking nicely on the leash can morph into pulling and yanking because people don't know how to prevent it.

How to Teach *Heel*

As always, you need a stash of treats in your pocket.

1. Put your Dachsie on a 6-foot (2-m) leash on your left side.
2. Say, "Heel."
3. Walk forward briskly so that your Dachsie knows which direction you're going.

Ask prospective trainers questions about their background and training philosophy.

As long as the leash has a comfortable U in it and your dog is even with your feet, keep walking.

4. When your Dachsie sprints ahead, stop. Eventually he'll return to you and sit. Be ready—you want this behavior.
5. The moment he does, say, "Yes," and reward him with a treat.
6. Begin walking again. As long as Dachsie walks in a line even with your feet— neither ahead of you nor behind—keep walking. When he sprints ahead, stop. When he wanders back, eventually he'll sit. Say, "Yes," and treat instantly.

It might take most of the afternoon to get across the yard or down the block, but that's okay. You're training your Dachsie to understand that there's no going ahead unless he walks at a level even with your feet. Practice, from this point, is a repetition of the *heel* sequence. After a few trials, play a short game or toss a ball for your Dachsie to retrieve. Then return to practice for another five minutes.

With your Dachsie, consistency is important. If you allow him to tug on the leash during your regular walks, you'll be teaching him that pulling on the leash is okay. You can't expect your Dachsie to heel on the leash some times and not others. If you want to allow him to the end of the leash, release him from *heel* and give a different command—perhaps "go play"—that means, "Go to the end of the leash and sniff around as you wish."

FINDING A PROFESSIONAL TRAINER

Whether you have a keen interest in learning all you can about training or you have a low confidence that you'll succeed with training on your own, try basic obedience classes. Before enrolling, however, find out about your prospective trainer.

A good trainer has lots of experience, references, and the ability to make you and your Dachsie feel comfortable. Sources for prospective trainers include your local Dachshund club and the following professional training organizations, which should have certified trainers nearby: the Association of Professional Dog Trainers (apdt.com), the Certification Council for Professional Dog Trainers (ccpdt.org), and the National Association of Dog Obedience Instructors (nadoi.org).

When you've identified several trainers who may match your needs, talk with each and arrange to observe a class they are teaching. Ask about the professional organizations they belong to, how long they have been training, and their training philosophy. If you don't feel comfortable with the answers before you start training, things will not improve when you get to class. If necessary, drive farther to get the trainer you would like to have. Trainers who get the best results are those who use positive reinforcement as the basis for their teaching.

CHAPTER
8

SOLVING PROBLEMS
WITH YOUR
DACHSHUND

Dachshunds who develop problem behaviors may need more physical and mental stimulation.

Problem behaviors are anything the human companion perceives to be unhelpful at the time the dog "does it." Most problem behaviors are repeated until the companion understands the reasons for them and addresses them.

CAUSES OF PROBLEM BEHAVIORS

Dogs exhibit problem behaviors for many reasons, but four are universal: (1) lack of exercise, (2) poor training, (3) inappropriate human body language, and (4) human misinterpretation of the dog's actions. Each of these problems comes from the human companion's lack of knowledge.

Dogs are different species. They have needs and means of communication that you must learn. As you do, you'll find the problems reduce in number and frequency. Learning about your dog is a lifelong quest, but if you continue to read and get advice from good sources, you and your dog will be happier and healthier.

Professional dog trainers have a saying: "A tired dog is a good dog." The fact is that most dogs don't get enough physical or mental stimulation. A Dachshund requires generous walks each day, along with the companionship you promised when you brought him into your home. Daily physical exercise for you and your dog will establish a good basis for addressing unwanted behaviors. Your Dachsie doesn't understand that you have other responsibilities. He understands that he is lonely and you're ignoring him.

When a Dachsie misbehaves, many companions believe that their dog is punishing them. Although you may feel that way, you are reading into your Dachsie's actions an intent that isn't there. He does what he does because he wants to and because you're not doing anything to interrupt his actions. Dogs don't seek to punish, embarrass, or make your life difficult. Dogs are the ultimate Zen creatures. They take each behavioral transaction with you and conduct it based on their previous training and experience. They don't plan, and they don't seek revenge.

SOLVING PROBLEM BEHAVIORS

Solving a problem behavior requires two components. First, the companion must address the reason that their dog is exhibiting the problem behavior. This means attending to all of the causes on a consistent basis. Dogs need guidance, and every interaction with a dog is a test. You, as the behavior director, must be consistent, firm, and loving.

Second, the companion has to work diligently with her dog to "break the habit" of, say, house soiling or excessive barking. If you see that your Dachsie is beginning a behavior pattern that is destructive, you should interrupt it. For example, if your dog always jumps up on visitors, you might leash him before the visitor enters and place your foot over the leash, leaving your dog plenty of room to stand but no leeway to jump. However, most of the time, companions can't tell when the pattern is about to start. Human beings are not nearly as good at reading dog body language as dogs are at reading human body language.

The most common problem behaviors include excessive barking, chewing, digging, house soiling, jumping, and nipping or biting. The most difficult part about these behaviors is that by the time you must do something about them, you're emotionally overwhelmed and your dog has now formed a habit that will take at least two weeks of intense effort to reform. Some behaviors take longer to eliminate. Some behaviors you cannot eliminate—Dachshunds, for example, were bred to dig, so this is an ingrained behavior. However, you can work to prevent dangerous outcomes of digging, such as escaping from an enclosure.

BARKING

Barking, a normal behavior, becomes a problem when your Dachsie barks excessively and inappropriately. Examples include continuous barking while in the backyard, barking at you, barking while in the car, and barking at every passing person. Not only is excessive barking a problem for you, but your neighbors will also have a problem with your Dachsie's barkfests. Excessive barking is *the* major reason that dogs lose their homes.

Excessive or inappropriate barking usually needs a response on several levels because your Dachsie's habit often results from several causes. Sometimes your Dachsie has a legitimate reason for barking, but other times he may believe

PUPPY POINTER

"The most important things you can do to raise a wonderful dog include [the following]: Have clear and consistent house rules, including what your puppy must do to earn the things he wants; provide lots of positive socialization, starting no later than 12 weeks of age; supervise to prevent bad habits from developing, and when you can't supervise, use a kennel; get the puppy comfortable spending some time alone; and seek help with any problems before they become entrenched. Puppies don't outgrow bad habits—you have to teach them alternatives."

—Kirsten Nielsen, PhD,
Certified Pet Dog Trainer, Portland, OR

that he can get what he wants because he has been "rewarded" in the past for barking—you've given him your attention, for example. Whatever the reason, your Dachsie is not getting enough guidance, and the barking may be creating a serious problem with your neighbors.

MEET YOUR DACHSHUND'S NEEDS

If you're the sort of person who gets sidetracked, your Dachsie may bark to say, "Hey, I've been asking to go outside for ten minutes. Help." Or, "Dinnertime was two hours ago. Put down that paintbrush and feed me." Whether you're at home or in the car, your dog may have legitimate reasons for barking until you pay attention, such as needing to empty his bladder or drink some water. In your Dachsie's world, these are emergencies. Examine your conscience. If this is you, set up reminders on your cell phone. Your Dachsie, who would rather risk your wrath barking than potty in the corner, will thank you.

STOP REWARDING BARKING

When your Dachsie knows the rules, he will follow them, but you must be consistent and not reward him for rule breaking. To stop rewarding barking is difficult because the big reward for your Dachsie is your attention. Negative attention, he figures, is better than nothing.

For example, a stranger comes to the door. Your tiny Dachsie barks. You say, "Stop barking." He continues. You pick up your Dachsie and cuddle him to keep him from annoying the stranger. For your Dachsie, you've just rewarded his barking. Now he knows that whenever a stranger comes to the door and you open it, if he keeps barking, you will pick him up and cuddle him. Make sense?

So now that you've trained him to bark, how can you untrain him? You have several choices. When the doorbell rings, you can take your Dachsie to his crate, give him a toy smeared with peanut butter, and then go answer the door. You gave him something better to do. You can also use a distraction, such as having him perform a basic command, until you teach him not to bark.

ENLIST YOUR NEIGHBORS' COOPERATION

If your Dachshund is barking enough to bother you, let your neighbors know that you're aware of the issue and you're working on it. The first thing you need to do is determine when and for how long your dog barks and what's causing him to bark. Ask your neighbors, walk around the block and listen for a while, or start a tape recorder or video camera when you leave for work.

If your Dachshund is barking enough to bother you, let your neighbors know that you're working on the issue.

NEVER USE A BARK COLLAR

Bark collars are designed to deliver something unpleasant (an aversive) whenever your Dachsie barks. The drawback is that bark collars don't address the cause. Usually, your Dachsie will stop barking, but he will develop a substitute behavior, such as digging or becoming destructive or aggressive. In addition, if barking is due to fear, use of a bark collar will make the fear worse.

If your Dachsie's barking is significant enough that you're considering a bark collar, call a trainer. (If your trainer recommends one of these collars while you work on the underlying problem, you should probably consider someone else.) Nine times out of ten, increased attention, exercise, and not rewarding your Dachsie's barking will solve the problem.

CHEWING

Chewing is a normal puppy behavior, but older dogs also have a need to chew. When your dog selects something inappropriate to chew—let's say a shoe—chewing becomes a problem. So the problem isn't chewing but selecting appropriate objects for chewing, like a toy instead of the shoe. Solve inappropriate chew toy selection through prevention, training, and consistent correction.

Provide your chewing Dachshund with attractive, acceptable chew toys so that he won't feel compelled to chew other things.

Your Dachsie's inappropriate selection of items is usually caused by more than one problem. For example, he may (a) have access to more space than he can responsibly handle, (b) have too few items he's allowed to chew, (c) be bored without enough exercise, and (d) not understand what he's forbidden to chew.

CURTAIL ROAMING

When your Dachsie isn't being supervised, curtail his ability to roam. Use baby gates, an exercise pen, or a crate. (You wouldn't let your two-year-old have full run of the house, would you?)

PROVIDE CHEW TOYS

Provide your Dachsie with acceptable chew toys. If he's teething, try a toy that includes something frozen to relieve his sore gums. If he has marvelous things to chew, why look for shoes? In the meantime, get out the treat ball and have your Dachsie work for his meals. Repeat after me: "A tired Dachshund is a good Dachshund."

PREVENT CHEWING OF IMMOVABLE OBJECTS

If the object is a window ledge or table leg, first restrict your Dachsie's access using baby gates. Otherwise, put him on a leash. When you forget (and you will) and he goes to chew, say, "No," give him an acceptable object to chew, and put up the barrier. Apply a bad-tasting spray, such as bitter apple, to the object. If your Dachsie chews nothing else, consider whether there may be a smell associated with the object that you don't perceive. In that case, you may have to remove the object altogether.

WHEN PREVENTION FAILS

When your Dachsie finds a shoe, take the shoe and give a firm "no." Then present an acceptable chew object. If your Dachshund takes off with his prize, never chase him. This makes stealing the object even more thrilling. Instead, make the space smaller by closing doors and putting up gates. Gather a leash and a treat to exchange for the treasured object.

When the space is small enough that your Dachshund doesn't try to run, put him on leash. Tell him, "Drop it," or "Give," whichever command you prefer. When you get the object, give your Dachsie a treat for complying (however reluctantly).

Put the forbidden object away and take your Dachsie on a short walk in the backyard, or outside. Give him a bit of exercise, a change of scenery, and when you return, give him something to chew in a space that contains nothing

Dachsies were bred to dig, but you can manage the behavior to keep your backyard intact.

"forbidden." You may need to keep irresistible objects—like your most expensive shoes—in the closet.

DIGGING

Dachshunds were bred to dig; you will never eliminate their desire to engage in this activity. What you can do is manage where they dig.

HOW TO MANAGE DIGGING

Let your Dachsie dig where his digging doesn't matter. If you have a farm, take him on a leash out to a place that's appropriate to dig and let him at it. This is where you bury his favorite toy and let him dig. Do this on bath day, since you'll be working hard to clean those paws, his underbelly, his face . . . well, you get the idea.

Some families of digging dogs build a backyard pit in which they put toys with treats to encourage them to dig in that one special place. Until you have the rules established, you'll be taking your Dachsie to the backyard on a long leash so that you stay in control. When he begins to dig in the wrong location, a "no" and moving your dog to the location where he is allowed to dig will get results. If you ignore your Dachsie's digging in unpermitted territory, you're asking for trouble.

By the way, if your Dachsie digs, you can't leave him in the yard without you— he'll dig under the fence. Alternatively, create a fenced cement run so that you have an outdoor spot that your Dachsie can't dig. And remember, a well-exercised Dachsie will be less driven to dig from boredom.

HOUSE SOILING

House soiling can be a difficult problem to solve. If an accident closely follows a successful potty trip or your dog is drinking excessive amounts of water, call your veterinarian. Your Dachsie may have worms or another intestinal problem that causes his behavior.

Likewise, when an older dog suddenly has trouble with his toileting, this is an indication of a health problem. If, however, you've just adopted an older dog, don't assume that he was ever potty trained, and remember that adoption is a stressful event either way. Your dog may be confused about where to go and how to ask in his new home.

For dogs in their long-established homes, travel and changes in routine and diet often cause accidents. Medications, especially antibiotics, also cause toileting problems.

NEVER PUNISH YOUR DOG

Do not punish your dog for "accidents." Never take him to the spot and give a verbal punishment. He doesn't know what you mean. The only appropriate verbal correction is to give a strong "Aaah aaah!" when you catch a dog mid-pee or mid-poop in the wrong place. The correction interrupts the flow. Take your

Dog Tale

"I have struggled with my shy Dachsie who lies down and urinates. The best thing you can do for the dog is not to make him feel that he needs to express submission to your authority. If you yell at a dog with this problem, you'll make it worse. Instead, always speak in a gentle tone . . . avoid looking directly at the dog when greeting him. When you want to reach down to pet him, don't bend over . . . crouch down, not facing the dog, and call him over, and pet without looking at him directly. If the dog starts to flip over or pee as you reach to pet, stand up and walk away so that the dog associates what he was doing with a removal of your attention."

—Holly Deeds, Dachshund trainer and teacher, Chattanooga, TN, and her heavily titled pack: FC Duchwood Great Expectations ("Stella"); FC Doxikota Our Mutual Friend ("Jenny"); and Doxikota's Copperfield Miss ("Lark")

dog immediately to his potty spot outside and give your "potty" command. (See Chapter 7.) When done, praise your dog lavishly.

CLEAN UP THOROUGHLY

When there has been an indoor incident, clean the spot thoroughly with soap and water and then use an enzyme cleaner to remove the smell. This will help prevent your dog from returning to the same spot. Next, return to a routine of frequent supervised trips outdoors. Even if you have a backyard, take your dog out on leash to be sure that you monitor his toileting. Take him to a particular spot and praise for performance.

ADHERE TO A SCHEDULE

Write down the schedule your dog keeps normally and take him out at these prescribed times, whether he asks to go out or not. Dogs usually eliminate feces a half hour or so after anything goes into their stomachs. When they drink water, they will soon need to potty.

Until you solve the problem, be rigorous about adhering to a schedule. You want to understand whether illness is causing the problem or whether some kind of upset has triggered inattentive toileting. During this period, *immediately* respond to his requests to go outside; otherwise, he may stop making them and hide his potty mistakes until you find them hours or days later.

JUMPING UP

Jumping up is having your Dachsie's front two feet leave the floor in an effort to get closer to the person's face to say hello. Guests and people on the street don't think this behavior is cute, and neither should you. Elderly people as well as those afraid of dogs are at risk of injury. If you allow this behavior, you're telling your Dachsie that you approve.

Trainer Kirsten Nielsen suggests that to correct a "jump up" problem, you must do your best to prevent the behavior and consistently correct every infraction so that the dog never gets petting or attention unless all four paws are on the ground.

WHILE WALKING ON LEASH

The best prevention is for you to have your dog sit while you stand on the slack of the leash so that when he gets up, he can stand comfortably. However, if he tries to jump up, the leash will prevent him from getting his paws on you or someone else. Be sure to praise and pet him as long as all four feet are on the

floor; when he tries to jump, firmly say, "No," and look away. As soon as he stops jumping, start praising and then try petting again.

Practice tempting situations on leash regularly. Try to anticipate the situations when your dog is most likely to jump and put the leash on in advance and stand on it so that he can't practice the unwanted behavior.

WHILE UNLEASHED AT HOME

Never knee your Dachsie in the chest or try to shove him away. If he jumps to greet you, turn around, avoid eye contact, and refuse to acknowledge him until he calms and sits. Then say, "Good," and pet him.

RETRAINING ON GREETING GUESTS AT HOME

You can make your visitors' experience so much better by using a simple *sit–stay*. First, place your Dachshund in the *sit–stay*. Open the door to a friend or family member (briefed ahead of time), who does not acknowledge your dog. If your dog starts forward, correct with "no." When successful, reward. Repeat until your Dachshund stays while you admit your training assistant. Reward effusively when he remains sitting while your assistant comes in and sits.

OTHER HELPFUL TIPS

Cue your guests on what to expect and ask for their cooperation. Ask them not to speak to or pet your Dachshund until they are inside and his four feet are on the floor. Newcomers should not make eye contact with your dog until he is under control and should pet him only when he behaves. Always leash your dog in advance for added control. For families not ready to commit to behavior training, keep your Dachsie in his crate while guests enter and leave.

NIPPING

If your dog has closed his teeth on your skin, you have been nipped. Nipping may or may not be a part of a larger pattern of aggression that ends in unpredictable and unprovoked biting. Aggressive behavior includes deep growling, showing teeth and staring, standing tall with the hair on his shoulders pointing up and his tail straight up, and finally, actual biting. Aggressive behavior can be directed toward the dog's family, strangers, or other dogs, and any breed of dog can be aggressive, Dachshunds included.

A simple *sit–stay* can help keep your Dachshund from jumping up on guests.

Everyone in the
household should
respect your Dachsie's
space while he's eating.

TRAIN YOUR PUPPY

If your puppy nips in play, stand up and turn your back to him. If he's biting to get you to stop doing something, don't stop. Hold on until he calms and stops biting.

Puppies, despite popular lore, are not good mixes with small children. Small children can be too rough with puppies, and puppies' sharp teeth can hurt small children. Neither children nor puppies know how to behave with each other—a recipe for disaster. Many Dachsies have lost their homes because they have nipped at small children who were tugging their ears or tail. Responsible children from 10 to 12 years old can more reasonably interact with puppies.

EDUCATE YOUR FAMILY

Conflicting signals make most dogs anxious, and anxiety can evolve into aggression. A common example is a child taking a toy from a dog, crawling into his crate, or taking his food while he's eating. A dog shouldn't have to defend his food, his shelter (crate), or his possessions. Once a dog know the rules (you gave me the food, and only you can take the food), he follows them and expects that everyone else should too. He doesn't understand that "this is only a child."

Everyone in the household should be aware that taking a dog's food or bothering him while he's eating is the number-one cause of trouble. If you're not confident about your family's ability to adhere to this rule, feed your Dachsie inside his crate in a quiet corner where you can ensure that no one bothers him.

BE THE LEADER

Aggression can come from a lack of leadership at home or from dominance practices like "rolling your dog" to show him who is boss. That is, in fact, an excellent way to provoke a bite. Leadership is giving your dog boundaries and a schedule and having him stick to it. It's about generally not reacting to bad behavior and distracting him instead. It's about giving plenty of praise when the dog comes when called, sits, and does his *sit–stay* before he's allowed to eat his meals. These actions reinforce that you are the leader and your dog is your sidekick.

Some people believe that they don't have to have to insist that a small dog behave properly because "I can always pick him up and make him . . ." Not only is this not true, but it's also one reason that small dogs have a reputation for being snappish and uncooperative. They have not been treated as a companion dog; rather, they have been treated as a fashion accessory.

Establishing Leadership

You can establish leadership by controlling your Dachsie's whereabouts. Put him on a leash and tether him to you. Where you go, he goes. Next, take control of resources. Take away whatever resources your dog guards. If you have them, he can't guard them. You should control the food, playtime, toys, petting, praise, furniture. You've got it all. Everything is good. Controlling your Dachsie's whereabouts and resources takes the leadership from his paws and puts it in your hands, where it belongs. This gives you a way to start over with your dog.

Your Dachshund should also learn how to ask politely for what he wants. How exactly do you do this? First, gather up a meal's worth of kibble and put it in your treat bag attached to your waist. The object is to make your Dachshund ask for permission instead of just taking the food. When he pokes and paws your leg, ignore him. When he sits and looks at you, say, "Good," and give him a piece of kibble.

This asking for permission can be made an everyday practice. Don't pet your Dachshund when he pokes his nose at you—wait for him to calm down first. When he wants to go outside, wait for him to sit at the door. Say, "Good," give him some kibble, and out you go, together. Give him the potty command outside, and when he goes, say, "Good," with a piece of kibble as a reward. Doing what he's supposed to do and asking permission from you for things he wants is the new regime.

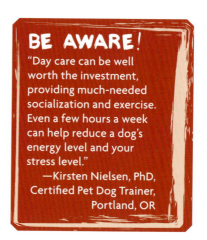

BE AWARE!

"Day care can be well worth the investment, providing much-needed socialization and exercise. Even a few hours a week can help reduce a dog's energy level and your stress level."

—Kirsten Nielsen, PhD, Certified Pet Dog Trainer, Portland, OR

WHEN TO SEEK PROFESSIONAL HELP

If you feel that your Dachsie is running the household, he probably is. That's when you need help altering his behavior. What can make a difficult situation even more

A professional trainer will help you to better understand your dog.

difficult is postponing professional help until the behavior conflicts become very unpleasant. If your dog behaves aggressively, call for help. You cannot handle this all on your own without expert guidance.

A professional trainer will guide you in the amount of exercise recommended to facilitate the training and on realistic step-by-step goals to correct your dog's behavior. Your trainer will show you what you're saying to your dog through your voice and posture. You may be very surprised at what you are saying through your body language! You may also be surprised at what your dog's body language says in return. Finally, a trainer will help you understand your Dachsie's intentions.

If you ever feel unsafe or concerned about being bitten, get help from a veterinary behavior specialist (avsabonline.org). If you suspect that your dog's behavior problems have a medical basis, consult a member of the American College of Veterinary Behaviorists (ACVB) (dacvb.org). These veterinarians can assess whether your dog's problems have a health-related cause or are behavioral only. In addition, they can recommend professionals to help you once the immediate "crisis" has passed.

SOLVING PROBLEMS WITH YOUR DACHSHUND

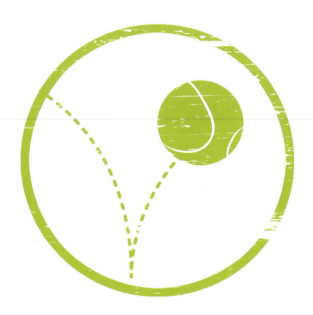

ACTIVITIES WITH YOUR DACHSHUND

Through sports and activities, you and your Dachsie can deepen your relationship.

Sports and activities that center on you and your Dachsie as a team not only cement the bond between you but also surround you with friends and professionals with like interests. You participate together, exercising your bodies, minds, and social skills. In addition, you learn from those with greater knowledge and skill, providing opportunities for you to grow together. Sports and activities provide you with opportunities to serve your club and your community, and through these experiences, you and your Dachsie deepen your relationship.

GETTING STARTED

Each sort of activity has its own information network. However, to get started learning more about Dachshund-centered activities in your area, try joining the Dachshund Club of America (DCA). Even if groups "aren't your thing," not only will you get acquainted with the variety of activities in your region, but you may also find a pal or two who share a common interest.

The DCA's quarterly newsletter—more a magazine than a newsletter—provides information on dog shows, field trials, breed rescue, and other activities that you might enjoy, along with a more national contact base that might be helpful to you. In addition, the DCA provides many other publications that can be a first step into Dachshund-related sports and activities.

SPORTS AND ACTIVITIES

Some of the activities you've always enjoyed will be more fun with your new best friend. Dachshunds regularly accompany their families in camping, walking, jogging, boating, and sightseeing. Because of their versatility and their sense of humor, Dachshunds can make your outings a bit more social and perhaps more comical. The Dachshund makes friends wherever he goes and seems to make a point of finding some trick or stunt to amuse his friends.

AGILITY

Agility is a sport made for Dachshunds' enthusiasm, energy, and brains. You've probably seen agility obstacles—jumps, slinky-like tunnels, A-frame ramps, teeter-totters, weave poles, the pause table, and others. In agility, a handler (you) directs her dog (Dachsie) through a specified order of these obstacles using movement, body language, and voice commands. Usually the course must be completed within a specified time.

Taught today using a technique called "targeting," agility dogs follow their owner's hand as it directs them through the obstacle course. The obstacles are height tailored to the dog's size and form a course that the owner memorizes. Handlers walk the approximately 100- by 100-foot (30.5- by 30.5-m) course, rehearsing their targeting moves. Then the dog–handler teams run the course, one after another.

Several organizations offer workshops to get you started. More advanced workshops help handlers upgrade their dog training skills and enhance their strategies for earning points in the unique scoring system. Although some people (and Dachshunds) thrive on the competition, most participants care only about the fun they are having. To find agility clubs in your area, consult apps.akc.org/apps/clubs/search. Additional groups specializing in agility include the United States Dog Agility Association, Inc. (USDAA) (usdaa.com), and the North American Dog Agility Council (NADAC) (nadac.com).

CONFORMATION (DOG SHOWS)

Many people are familiar with conformation events, such as Crufts and the Westminster Kennel Club Dog Show, that are televised. In addition to these well-known shows, hundreds of events take place around the world every weekend. Conformation events evaluate dogs' overall appearance and structure, which are indications of their ability to produce quality puppies.

Training dogs for conformation is more involved than it looks. Learning to handle your dog so that he can properly gait (show his movement) and stack

In agility, the handler directs her dog through obstacles using movement, body language, and voice commands.

(stand in a certain way that shows his physical conformation to best advantage) requires practice and skill. In addition, conformation classes require much more grooming than some other Dachshund-related activities. Those who compete generally love it. Workshops run by local Dachshund clubs help you learn the fundamentals of exhibiting your dog in these competitions and teach you grooming and handling skills.

So what's the competition about? Judges examine the dogs and give awards based on how closely each dog compares to the judge's mental image of the "perfect" dog described in the breed standard. Each dog is presented to a judge by its owner, breeder, or professional handler. The judge, an expert on the Dachshund certified by the sponsoring registry, chooses which dog best fits the standards for structure, temperament, and movement.

Deciding whether to show your Dachshund is something to consider before purchase because some dogs conform more closely to the standard than others. If conformation showing is an interest you have, discuss this with your breeder in advance.

CAMPING

An enthusiastic family member, your Dachsie wants to camp with you. If you're backpacking, no problem! You'll need your Dachsie's leash and a pack that contains his food, water, latrine trowel, fold-up water dish, and first-aid kit, along with a toy to keep him occupied at night. Oh, and don't forget to pack the extra camp towel to dry your Dachsie after swimming.

Before you head out, check your state park website to be sure that you select a trail that allows dogs. If you're going camping in an established campground, you can find a place where your Dachsie will be welcome near most places that you'll want to go. To find campgrounds that will accept your Dachsie, try petfriendlytravel.com/campgrounds. To plan more outings, consult your local bookstore. You might find some local reference books on outings and camping with dogs.

CANINE FREESTYLE

Canine freestyle is a choreographed performance of handler and dog set to music. Similar to ballroom dancing routines, canine freestyle creates an entertaining occasion for spectators with turns, pivots, and patterns, showing that handler and dog can train together simply to have fun. For more information, consult the Canine Freestyle Federation, Inc. (CFF) (canine-freestyle.org), and the American Kennel Club (AKC) (akc.org). Another organization with local freestyle groups is the World Canine Freestyle Organization (WCFO) (worldcaninefreestyle.org).

CANINE GOOD CITIZEN® TEST

The Canine Good Citizen (CGC) test, administered by the AKC, is a way your family can measure whether your Dachsie is ready to behave in regular community outings, is under control when he's on leash, and is not aggressive toward people or other dogs. It is also a great starting point for service-dog work or sporting events. Any Dachshund—young or old—who has received the basic immunizations is eligible.

The CGC test has ten parts, which involve your Dachsie minding you through basic commands and behaving well around other dogs and people. Individual test items include things like walking through crowds of people or other dogs, accepting a friendly stranger's approach and petting, and showing confidence with distractions.

Particularly for Dachshunds who have not been well socialized, CGC training is

PUPPY POINTER

Six months is the usual age to qualify for participating in any competition, even though most Dachshunds are not mature enough at that age to compete.

important, and achieving this level of training may take much longer for them than for Dachshunds starting as puppies. For their owners and others, CGC training classes can be eye-opening. Certification classes give adults or kids and their Dachshunds a set of tasks realistic to learn in six weeks. Dogs who finish their CGC certifications are better-trained family companions, comfortable in most situations. Earning this certification gives people confidence and encouragement to try other activities. For more information about the Canine Good Citizen program and related training in your area, consult akc.org/ dogowner/training/canine_good_citizen.

EARTHDOG

Earthdog work is what the Dachshund was bred to do. Both the AKC and the American Working Terrier Association (AWTA) hold earthdog trials (called "den trials" by the AWTA), in which the object is to identify a game tunnel and dig to reach the game, sometimes navigating obstacles in the process. Earthdog scents are often from wildlife, including badgers, rabbits, and foxes, but the game (or "quarry") in AKC earthdog tests are adult rats, protected in an enclosure inside the den and separated from the dogs by additional barriers. Food and water are provided for the rats during the trials. (No animals are injured in the pursuit of this sport.)

AKC and AWTA trials are open to both Dachshunds and terriers. What Dachshund would not want to participate in digging dens? To find a schedule of trials in a location near you, check akc.org/events/earthdog/ or awta.org/ services.html.

FIELD TRIALS

Field trials are intended to test the hunting ability of dogs. In other words, they are intended to exercise your Dachsie's natural inclination to scent and trail game. The field trial atmosphere is quite different from that of the confirmation show ring. The trials are held out of doors in locations and conditions that simulate those encountered in the real hunting field. During the competition, each dog must operate on his training and instinct, without assistance from any person.

If you've never seen a field trial, you're in for a treat. Once handlers release their dogs, the dogs work until the have scented the game, often a rabbit. Then the trailing begins. Preferable is lots of Dachsie "song," the beautiful sound the dogs make when they are on the scent and progress is being made. What makes the trials more amazing is that the dogs do the work themselves, without any signaling or direction from their handlers.

Field trials exercise your Dachshund's scenting and trailing capabilities.

Many people enjoy field trials and prepare their Dachsie for them starting when he is weaning. To learn about field trialing, contact your local Dachshund or Beagle club and attend the next event as an observer. You'll learn whether you and your Dachsie are interested in trying this sport yourselves. For more information, check apps.akc.org//classic/events/field_trials/dachshunds/index. cfm.

OBEDIENCE

Many owners and their Dachshunds begin obedience training in puppy kindergarten. In AKC obedience, dog-and-handler teams are judged on how closely they match the judge's idea of a perfect performance in completing a series of exercises. Obedience trials showcase well-trained dogs and give owners a chance to enjoy companionship. What is spectacular about obedience is that you can compete at many different levels, with the emphasis on the teamwork between a handler and her Dachshund.

The most basic level of competition is the Novice class. Here, dogs are expected to perform very simple commands, such as heeling and recall (or "come"). However, the more difficult tests of extended *sit*– and *down*– *stays* are also required to earn the Companion Dog (CD) title, the first on the obedience ladder. To earn the next higher-level title, Companion Dog Excellent (CDX), dogs must enter the Open class and meet significantly more difficult tests. These include retrieval of articles, hurdling, and working accurately on commands off leash. Utility-class trials offer the highest level of competition, adding scent discrimination, directed retrieves, and jumping and silent signal exercises. Dogs who succeed in these competitions can earn the Utility Dog (UD) title.

RALLY

Rally is a combination of obedience and agility, with a less "rigid" set of rules. Dog and handler complete a course designed by the rally judge. A sport in which everyone can compete on leash at a novice level, rally has scoring that is not as rigorous as obedience, and as in agility, you can talk to your dog. The rules can be found at akc.org/events/rally/index.cfm.

THERAPY WORK

Therapy organizations train volunteer pet–partner teams to do animal-assisted activities, such as "meet and greets," to brighten people's days. Teams also do therapy work with a licensed health care or human services provider to help

A Dachsie with a suitable temperament makes a great candidate for therapy work.

patients meet specific goals. The first step in any therapeutic training program is the Canine Good Citizen (CGC) certification. Once your Dachsie has passed this test, contact Pet Partners at petpartners.org.

TRACKING

Dachshunds have successfully participated in tracking competitions, which test the skills necessary for search-and-rescue work. AKC tracking competitions allow both handlers and their dogs to perfect their skills and have fun through competition and allow Dachshunds to do what they were bred to do—scent and track. For more information, see apps.akc.org/classic/events/tracking.

VERSATILITY

Proud of the Dachshund's versatility, the Dachshund Club of America (DCA) offers a versatility certificate program that combines conformation, field trials, obedience, rally, agility, earthdog, and tracking into a "heptathlon." Dachsie people who love keeping their dogs busy and well exercised and who love being with other Dachsie people will find this a fun way to allow their dogs to exercise all their skills. For more information, check out the DCA's versatility certificate handbook on their website.

WALKING AND JOGGING

You need no special equipment or locations to walk or run with your Dachsie. Just head outdoors with your best friend on the 6-foot (2-m) leash that's required in most metro and suburban areas and parks along with a few plastic bags so you can pick up after him. You may want to use your "hands-free" leash.

Leashes, by the way, aren't always about controlling your dog. They are there to put all dogs on an equal level when they meet. Leashes also accommodate people (and there are many) who are afraid of dogs, and they keep dogs from dashing into the street after a squirrel.

If you are walking or running at night, your Dachsie will also need a safety vest and a blinking light, just the way you do. Each of you needs to be visible, especially if you get separated. On dark, rainy nights, you will want cars, bicycles, and pedestrians to see you clearly.

For you long-distance walkers and runners, remember to build your Dachsie's endurance and pad calluses gradually. Puppies, who have not completed their growth and development, will not be ready to run as far or as fast as you can. And if your Dachsie has not been regularly exercised, build his endurance slowly.

Carry a ready supply of water for long runs, as dogs can't keep cool by sweating as humans can. Your Dachsie cools through panting, which increases water loss. Also, be a good sport and clean up after your dog. Nothing is more unsightly or unhealthy than sidewalks or parks full of dog waste. Dispose of waste in a trash can.

Dog Tale

Unwilling to do much after the death of his shorthaired companion of many years, the red Longhaired Dachshund Basil was definitely up for a car ride. Although that doesn't qualify as a "sport" for some dogs, Basil considered the ride an uplifting activity.

TRAVELING WITH YOUR DACHSIE

Sharing your lives sometimes means traveling together as a family. When the destination is dog friendly, your Dachsie will prefer to be with you. If your destination is Disney World, he won't be admitted, so he's going to remain at home.

TRAVEL BY CAR

To make it easy and safe to include your Dachsie on road trips, keep a crate in the car so that he can go whenever you do. Although your Dachsie will want to ride in your lap, this is unsafe. Unrestrained dogs not only cause distracted-driving accidents, but they can also injure themselves or other people traveling in your car.

Crates, which professionals use, have several advantages. Your dog and passengers will be safer, your Dachsie will have his "home away from home" for feelings of security and protection, and he will not chew through his restraint. Although car seats and seat harnesses allow your dog to appear to be more "free," he can (and will) chew through these restraints over and over again.

Once your crate is permanently stowed in the car, all you have to do is check out the list of dog-friendly attractions, parks, and camps that specialize in activities for people and their dogs. Dogfriendly.com, the best site on the web for dog travel—related information, provides locations for emergency veterinary services, pet-supply stores, overnight accommodations, and attractions that accept dogs.

TRAVEL BY AIR

Most dog folks are terrified to ship their dogs, and here's why: When weather or mechanical delays occur, things can get ugly fast. You have no control over

Walking and jogging are great ways to have fun with your Dachshund.

how long your dog might be sitting on the tarmac or under what conditions. If you have no alternative other than to ship your dog, find flights that are direct, even if you have to make a long drive to another airport.

If you're going with your dog, you have two choices: under-seat or in the luggage compartment. Depending on the size of your dog and the airline, you may have to fly with your Dachshund in the luggage compartment, which can be a very uncomfortable situation. Check with the airline to be sure that they have space available in temperature- and pressure-controlled cargo holds.

For Miniature Dachshunds, the flight situation is easier because they usually go under the seat. With airlines' increasing regulations and fees, know that you need to arrange in advance for your Mini Dachsie to fly in the passenger compartment. Most airlines limit the number of under-seat pets. In addition, each airline has different health rules. Bring your pet's health records no matter what the airline says. In some states, your dog's paperwork may be checked on arrival.

PET-FRIENDLY LODGING

The number of hotels that accept people with in-room pets is expanding. Motel 6 has been the standby for pet owners for years. Most La Quinta Inns allow pets as well. Some Best Western, Holiday Inn, Marriott, and high-end hotels also accept pets. Check dogfriendly.com for a list of hotels that might work for your next trip.

BE AWARE!
When you're traveling with more than one dog, give each a properly sized crate. Sharing a crate, even one that is large, is too much togetherness— even for good friends.

RESOURCES

ASSOCIATIONS AND ORGANIZATIONS

BREED CLUBS

American Kennel Club (AKC)
8051 Arco Corporate Drive,
Suite 100
Raleigh, NC 27617-3390
Telephone: (919) 233-9767
Fax: (919) 233-3627
E-Mail: info@akc.org
www.akc.org

Canadian Kennel Club (CKC)
200 Ronson Drive, Suite 400
Etobicoke, Ontario M9W 5Z9
Telephone: (416) 675-5511
Fax: (416) 675-6506
E-Mail: information@ckc.ca
www.ckc.ca

The Dachshund Club (UK)
Honorary Secretary: Mrs. Anne
Moore
E-Mail: romanchiwires@aol.com
www.dachshundclub.co.uk

Dachshund Club of America (DCA)
Corresponding Secretary: Cheryl
Shultz
E-Mail: cherevee@sbcglobal.net
www.dachshundclubofamerica.
org

Fédération Cynologique Internationale (FCI)
FCI Office
Place Albert 1er, 13
B – 6530 Thuin
Belgique
Telephone: +32 71 59.12.38
Fax: +32 71 59.22.29
www.fci.be

The Kennel Club (UK)
1-5 Clarges Street, Piccadilly,
London W1J 8AB
Telephone: 0844 463 3980
Fax: 020 7518 1028
www.thekennelclub.org.uk

National Miniature Dachshund Club (NMDC)
Secretary: Aubrey Nash
E-Mail: Aubray@aol.com
www.dachshund-nmdc.org

United Kennel Club (UKC)
100 E. Kilgore Road
Kalamazoo, MI 49002-5584
Telephone: (269) 343-9020
Fax: (269) 343-7037
www.ukcdogs.com

PET SITTERS

National Association of Professional Pet Sitters (NAPPS)
15000 Commerce Parkway, Suite C
Mt. Laurel, New Jersey 08054
Telephone: (856) 439-0324
Fax: (856) 439-0525
E-Mail: napps@petsitters.org
www.petsitters.org

Pet Sitters International
201 East King Street
King, NC 27021-9161
Telephone: (336) 983-9222
Fax: (336) 983-5266
E-Mail: info@petsit.com
www.petsit.com

RESCUE ORGANIZATIONS AND ANIMAL WELFARE GROUPS

American Humane Association
1400 16th Street NW, Suite 360
Washington, DC 20036
Telephone: (800) 227-4645
E-Mail: info@americanhumane.org
www.americanhumane.org

American Society for the Prevention of Cruelty to Animals (ASPCA)
424 E. 92nd Street
New York, NY 10128-6804
Telephone: (212) 876-7700
www.aspca.org

Royal Society for the Prevention of Cruelty to Animals (RSPCA)
RSPCA Advice Team
Wilberforce Way
Southwater
Horsham
West Sussex
RH13 9RS
United Kingdom
Telephone: 0300 1234 999
www.rspca.org.uk

SPORTS
International Agility Link (IAL)
85 Blackwall Road
Chuwar, Queensland
Australia 4306
Telephone: 61 (07) 3202 2361
Fax: 61 (07) 3281 6872
E-Mail: steve@agilityclick.com
www.agilityclick.com/~ial/

The North American Dog Agility Council (NADAC)
24605 Dodds Rd.
Bend, Oregon 97701
www.nadac.com

North American Flyball Association (NAFA)
1333 West Devon Avenue, #512
Chicago, IL 60660
Telephone: (800) 318-6312
Fax: (800) 318-6312
E-Mail: flyball@flyball.org
www.flyball.org

United States Dog Agility Association (USDAA)
P.O. Box 850955
Richardson, TX 75085
Telephone: (972) 487-2200
Fax: (972) 231-9700
www.usdaa.com

The World Canine Freestyle Organization, Inc.
P.O. Box 350122
Brooklyn, NY 11235
Telephone: (718) 332-8336
Fax: (718) 646-2686
E-Mail: WCFODOGS@aol.com
www.worldcaninefreestyle.org

THERAPY
Pet Partners
875 124th Ave, NE, Suite 101
Bellevue, WA 98005
Telephone: (425) 679-5500
Fax: (425) 679-5539
E-Mail: info@petpartners.org
www.petpartners.org

Therapy Dogs Inc.
P.O. Box 20227
Cheyenne, WY 82003
Telephone: (877) 843-7364
Fax: (307) 638-2079
E-Mail: therapydogsinc@
qwestoffice.net
www.therapydogs.com

Therapy Dogs International (TDI)
88 Bartley Road
Flanders, NJ 07836
Telephone: (973) 252-9800
Fax: (973) 252-7171
E-Mail: tdi@gti.net
www.tdi-dog.org

TRAINING
American College of Veterinary Behaviorists (ACVB)
College of Veterinary Medicine,
4474 TAMU
Texas A&M University
College Station, Texas 77843-4474
www.dacvb.org

American Kennel Club Canine Health Foundation, Inc. (CHF)
P. O. Box 900061
Raleigh, NC 27675
Telephone: (888) 682-9696
Fax: (919) 334-4011
www.akcchf.org

Association of Professional Dog Trainers (APDT)
104 South Calhoun Street
Greenville, SC 29601
Telephone: (800) PET-DOGS
Fax: (864) 331-0767
E-Mail: information@apdt.com
www.apdt.com

International Association of Animal Behavior Consultants (IAABC)
565 Callery Road
Cranberry Township, PA 16066
E-Mail: info@iaabc.org
www.iaabc.org

National Association of Dog Obedience Instructors (NADOI)
7910 Picador Drive
Houston, TX 77083-4918
Telephone: (972) 296-1196
E-Mail: info@nadoi.org
www.nadoi.org

VETERINARY AND HEALTH RESOURCES

The Academy of Veterinary Homeopathy (AVH)
P. O. Box 232282
Leucadia, CA 92023-2282
Telephone: (866) 652-1590
Fax: (866) 652-1590
www.theavh.org

American Academy of Veterinary Acupuncture (AAVA)
P.O. Box 1058
Glastonbury, CT 06033
Telephone: (860) 632-9911
www.aava.org

American Animal Hospital Association (AAHA)
12575 W. Bayaud Ave.
Lakewood, CO 80228
Telephone: (303) 986-2800
Fax: (303) 986-1700
E-Mail: info@aahanet.org
www.aahanet.org

American College of Veterinary Internal Medicine (ACVIM)
1997 Wadsworth Blvd., Suite A
Lakewood, CO 80214-5293
Telephone: 303-231-9933
Telephone (US or Canada): (800) 245-9081
Fax: (303) 231-0880
E-Mail: ACVIM@ACVIM.org
www.acvim.org

American College of Veterinary Ophthalmologists (ACVO)
P.O. Box 1311
Meridian, ID 83860
Telephone: (208) 466-7624
Fax: (208) 466-7693
E-Mail: office13@acvo.com
www.acvo.org

American Heartworm Society (AHS)
P.O. Box 8266
Wilmington, DE 19803-8266
E-Mail: info@heartwormsociety.org
www.heartwormsociety.org

American Holistic Veterinary Medical Association (AHVMA)
P. O. Box 630
Abingdon, MD 21009-0630
Telephone: (410) 569-0795
Fax: (410) 569-2346
E-Mail: office@ahvma.org
www.ahvma.org

American Veterinary Medical Association (AVMA)
1931 North Meacham Road, Suite 100
Schaumburg, IL 60173-4360
Telephone: (800) 248-2862
Fax: (847) 925-1329
www.avma.org

ASPCA Animal Poison Control Center
Telephone: (888) 426-4435
www.aspca.org

British Veterinary Association (BVA)
7 Mansfield Street
London
W1G 9NQ
Telephone: 020 7636 6541
Fax: 020 7908 6349
E-Mail: bvahq@bva.co.uk
www.bva.co.uk

Canine Eye Registration Foundation (CERF)
P.O. Box 199
Rantoul, Il 61866-0199
Telephone: (217) 693-4800
Fax: (217) 693-4801
E-Mail: CERF@vmdb.org
www.vmdb.org

Orthopedic Foundation for Animals (OFA)
2300 E. Nifong Boulevard
Columbia, MO 65201-3806
Telephone: (573) 442-0418
Fax: (573) 875-5073
E-Mail: ofa@offa.org
www.offa.org

US Food and Drug Administration Center for Veterinary Medicine (CVM)
7519 Standish Place
HFV-12
Rockville, MD 20855
Telephone: (240) 276-9300
E-Mail: AskCVM@fda.hhs.gov
www.fda.gov/AnimalVeterinary/

PUBLICATIONS
BOOKS
Ewing, Susan M. *The Dachshund.* With consulting veterinary editor Wayne Hunthausen, DVM. Neptune City: TFH Publications, 2005.

Libby, Tracy. *High-Energy Dogs.* TFH Publications, Inc., 2009.

Swager, Peggy. *Training the Hard-to-Train Dog.* TFH Publications, Inc., 2009.

Wood, Deborah. *Little Dogs.* TFH Publications, Inc., 2004.

MAGAZINES
AKC Family Dog
American Kennel Club
260 Madison Avenue
New York, NY 10016
Telephone: (800) 490-5675
E-Mail: familydog@akc.org
www.akc.org/pubs/familydog

AKC Gazette
American Kennel Club
260 Madison Avenue
New York, NY 10016
www.akc.org/pubs/gazette/digital_edition.cfm

WEBSITES
Nylabone
www.nylabone.com

TFH Publications, Inc.
www.tfh.com

INDEX

Note: **Boldface** numbers indicate illustrations.

DEDICATION

This book is dedicated to the many friends of Dachshunds.

ACKNOWLEDGMENTS

Thank you to Stephanie Fornino, Matthew Haviland, Terry Albert, Holly Deeds, Andrea Hurst, Dr. Kirsten Nielsen, Kathy Dorman, Jill Kessler Miller, Georganne Duron, Dr. Patricia J. Luttgen, Gail Parker, Dr. Sophia Yin, the American Animal Hospital Association (AAHA), the American Holistic Veterinary Medical Association (AHVMA), the Dachshund Club of America (DCA), and the American Kennel Club (AKC).

ABOUT THE AUTHOR

Writer and educator **Carol Frischmann** has been fascinated by pets, nature, and science since she was saved in a childhood accident by the family dog. After earning a BS in Science Education at Duke University, she pursued her love of animals by educating visitors at zoos and museums and by writing books and for magazines, newspapers, and pet columns. Now teaching at the Grand Canyon School and living inside the national park, Carol and her parrots are often visited by their many Dachshund friends.

PHOTO CREDITS

Africa Studio (Shutterstock.com): 113
a katz (Shutterstock.com): 126
Alexander Raths (Shutterstock.com): 80, 85
Alfred Nesswetha (Shutterstock.com): 60
alvant (Shutterstock.com): 103
Artem and Olga Sapegin (Shutterstock.com): 82
Brent Hofacker (Shutterstock.com): 46
chris kolaczan (Shutterstock.com): 55
clesimo (Shutterstock.com): 131
creativex (Shutterstock.com): 7
Csanad Kiss (Shutterstock.com): 56
dien (Shutterstock.com): 52
dogboxstudio (Shutterstock.com): 24, 29, 36, 63, 94, 105, 135
DragoNika (Shutterstock.com): 48, 53
Ekaterina Kamenetsky (Shutterstock.com): 38
Eric Isselee (Shutterstock.com): 8, 79
Erik Lam (Shutterstock.com): back cover, 1
Evan Fariston (Shutterstock.com): 43
flywish (Shutterstock.com): 73
Hannamariah (Shutterstock.com): 16, 28, 62, 97, 116

Horiyan (Shutterstock.com): 3
igor.stevanovic (Shutterstock.com): 76, 123
Inna Astakhova (Shutterstock.com): 101
iVangelos (Shutterstock.com): 114
Jagodka (Shutterstock.com): front cover
Jennay Hitesman (Shutterstock.com): 98
Kirstin Pold (Shutterstock.com): 12
KPG_Payless (Shutterstock.com): 58
KPG Payless2 (Shutterstock.com): 10, 88, 90
kuban_girl (Shutterstock.com): 4
leungchopan (Shutterstock.com): 6, 77
Liliya Kulianionak (Shutterstock.com): 14, 26
Lisa F. Young (Shutterstock.com): 119
Marika San (Shutterstock.com): 106
Mark Herreid (Shutterstock.com): 128
michaelstephan-fotografie (Shutterstock.com): 50
Mikkel Bigandt (Shutterstock.com): 108
mykeyruna (Shutterstock.com): 66

Nikolai Tsvetkov (Shutterstock.com): 83
pingu2004 (Shutterstock.com): 18
Poprotskiy Alexey (Shutterstock.com): 70
Richard Chaff (Shutterstock.com): 57
Sean Locke Photography (Shutterstock.com): 74
Soloviova Liudmyla (Shutterstock.com): 23
Sonja Calovini (Shutterstock.com): 65
steamroller_blues (Shutterstock.com): 44
Suponev Vladimir (Shutterstock.com): 9
takayuki (Shutterstock.com): 92
Tasha Karidis (Shutterstock.com): 68
Tatyana Vyc (Shutterstock.com): 40
Vitalinka (Shutterstock.com): 11
VKarlov (Shutterstock.com): 21
WilleeCole Photography (Shutterstock.com): 13, 32, 54, 120, 121
YasenElena77 (Shutterstock.com): 132
Ysbrand Cosijn (Shutterstock.com): 39
Zanna Holstova (Shutterstock.com): 110, 124

ABOUT ANIMAL PLANET™

Animal Planet™ is the only television network dedicated exclusively to the connection between humans and animals. The network brings people of all ages together by tapping into our fundamental fascination with animals through an array of fresh programming that includes humor, competition, drama, and spectacle from the animal kingdom.

ABOUT *DOGS 101*

The most comprehensive—and most endearing—dog encyclopedia on television, *DOGS 101* spotlights the adorable, the feisty and the unexpected. A wide-ranging rundown of everyone's favorite dog breeds—from the Dalmatian to Xoloitzcuintli —this series surveys a variety of breeds for their behavioral quirks, genetic history, most famous examples and wildest trivia. Learn which dogs are best for urban living and which would be the best fit for your family. Using a mix of animal experts, pop-culture footage and stylized dog photography, *DOGS 101* is an unprecedented look at man's best friend.

At Animal Planet,
we're committed to providing
quality products designed to
help your pets live long,
healthy, and happy lives.